Remembering our Fallen

Remembering the men of
Howden-le-Wear and Fir Tree
who gave their lives during the
Great War of 1914 - 1918

**Researched and compiled
by members of the
Howden-le-Wear Local
History Society**

Dedication

**To the memory of those with links to
Howden-le-Wear and Fir Tree
who gave their lives during the
Great War
that we might live in freedom**

This book has been funded through a grant generously provided by the Heritage Lottery Fund and will be made available to the residents of Howden-le-Wear and Fir Tree free of charge.

Cover pictures: The poppies in the images on the front and back covers of the book were handmade by the members of the Howden-le-Wear Craft Group in 2014 to commemorate 100 years since the beginning of the Great War.

Published by Howden-le-Wear History Society and 'Relativity'

First Edition: March 2015

ISBN 978-0-9571257-2-8

To the best of the researchers' knowledge, the information in this book is accurate but, if readers wish to make comment, they can contact the Howden-le-Wear History Society.

Further copies of this book may be obtained from Howden-le-Wear History Society which can be contacted through emailing

Howden-le-Wearhistorysociety@hotmail.co.uk

Printed by **B&B Press (Parkgate) Ltd**.
Aldwarke Road,
Rotherham
South Yorkshire
S62 6DY

FOREWORD

In April 2013, I gave a presentation to Howden-le-Wear History Society about the book I had written called 'Witton Warriors' which told the story of the men from the neighbouring village of Witton-le-Wear who gave their lives during the Great War. It also included information about their families and the social history of the era. At the end of the talk, I said that I hoped I had inspired them to research the stories of the men named on the Howden-le-Wear War Memorial and, if they wanted any advice or support, they only had to ask. Little did I appreciate what the next year would bring!

Six months later I received a call asking if I could come along to a meeting in early January 2014 to give some support to a group of members who wished to research the stories of the men from Howden-le-Wear. At the meeting it became clear that they wished me to lead the project and, because I am passionate about the recording of local history, I agreed to help.

2014 proved to be a very busy and productive year. The project group members learned many new skills researching the families and the military records, and each member brought differing expertise to the group.

I found myself in the very privileged position of becoming editor of the collated information, and recognised very quickly what a special written memorial this would become. Preparing the first draft of the book and sharing it with all the members was a daunting process, but the constructive criticism received, as well as the grammatical corrections, have all ensured that the final outcome is a book that we can all be proud of.

I hope readers appreciate the stories of the people of the two villages and acknowledge the wonderful resource they have in the members of Howden-le-Wear History Society.

Anne Yuill

War Memorial at Howden-le-Wear on the 11th November 2014. It was unveiled on the 11th November 1924 by Captain R .A. Howe of Willington. The knitted poppies around the Memorial were made by the ladies of Howden-le-Wear Craft Group.

Image courtesy of Kathleen Parkin

Children of Howden-le-Wear c1900. Some of these children may have been the men who became servicemen or wives of servicemen who served during the Great War.
Image courtesy of Howden-le-Wear History Society

Bridge Street, Howden-le-Wear, following the rebuilding of the Primitive Methodist Chapel in 1904.
Image courtesy of Howden-le-Wear History Society

❖ *INTRODUCTION*

The idea for this book came about when members of Howden-le-Wear History Society wanted to know more about the servicemen from The Great War whose names appear on the village stone War Memorial obelisk that is situated in the centre of the village at the crossing of Bridge Street and High Street. It had been unveiled on the 11th November 1924 by Captain R. A. Howe of Willington.

This is not the only memorial in Howden-le-Wear. After the end of the war, the organist of St Mary the Virgin Parish Church in Howden-le-Wear decided to produce a Roll of Honour on parchment with the approval of the local vicar. Unfortunately, the Church authorities were upset that the work had been completed without official design or inscription approval, but the Roll of Honour was eventually allowed to hang within the church.

St Mary the Virgin Church, the Parish Church for Howden-le-Wear and Fir Tree. *Image courtesy of Howden-le-Wear History Society*

After 1945, the parchment Roll of Honour in the church was replaced by a wooden memorial which also included the names of those men lost during the 1939 - 1945 conflict. When St Mary the Virgin Parish Church was closed and deconsecrated in 2008, the History Society was offered both the Roll of Honour and the wooden memorial, which are now in its archives. There are, however, some discrepancies between the details on the Roll of Honour and the wooden memorial board, and further research has shown that the parchment memorial has the more accurate information.

Howden-le-Wear was a tight knit community 100 years ago. The men worked in the local mines, pipe works, farms or other local industry. The women stayed at home to look after their large families, and shopping was done in the village or Crook, two miles away.

Howden-le-Wear Council School in the early 1900s.
Image courtesy of Howden-le-Wear History Society

Schools were local with children attending school until the age of 14 unless they went to a Grammar School which was fee paying or entry by scholarships. Churches and chapels played a major part in people's lives and social activities all took place in the local area. People in Howden-le-Wear were lucky as they had a superb railway station, and day trips to Durham, Bishop Auckland, Darlington and even Saltburn were among the treats of the day.

Mr Turnbull, head teacher, and pupils 1918 - 1920.
Image courtesy of Howden-le-Wear History Society

The men who enlisted in the services during the war were well known to one another and their families knew everyone. This meant that, when a death occurred to one of our own, it affected not only the immediate family but the whole village. This was the emphasis that the project group wanted to highlight when they came together in early 2014. Members had varied reasons why they chose which servicemen they wished to research; some knew the family, some had the same surname, and some just wanted to help. The members were:

Mike Abbott, Alan Brian, Irene Brian, Chris Gibson, Christine Gibson, Frances Ann Johnson, David Marshall, Helen Morton, Kathleen Parkin, Tom Parkin, Joan Potts and **Anne Yuill.**

The research information was collated and forms the text of this book, while the individual style of writing of each of the researchers has been maintained.

Once the project group was established, **John Alderson** from Fir Tree was invited to join in to enable the information from Fir Tree War Memorial to be included within the book. The two villages are interlinked through proximity and the local mines and industry, as well as being in the same Parish.

A grant was awarded from the Heritage Lottery Fund which has enabled the book to be produced and given free of charge to residents of Howden-le-Wear and Fir Tree.

Howden-le-Wear History Society is deeply indebted to many of the relatives of the servicemen who have freely given information and photographs to increase knowledge of the individual families. They were:

Anthea Agar, **Joyce Charlton**, **William Clark**, **Billy Coates**, **Myra Griffiths**, **Sue Heslop**, **Douglas Kavanagh**, **Dorothy Longstaff**, **the Nutley Family** and **Ellis Williams**.

To the best of our knowledge, the information contained within this book is accurate. If anyone notices any discrepancies, please contact Howden-le-Wear History Society by email at:

Howden-le-Wearhistorysociety@hotmail.co.uk

The researchers have filtered the information used in the book, but have developed a very extensive database and, should anyone desire more information on individual servicemen, please make contact.

We hope you find the book informative and interesting and, by writing down these stories, we hope that in our small way we have helped to value their sacrifice.

Members of Howden-le-Wear Local History Society

February 2015

❖ *HOWDEN-LE-WEAR & DISTRICT 1914 - 1918*

At the start of the 20th century, many Victorian traits remained and this was still evident in many aspects of life in 1914. Howden-le-Wear was a relatively self-sufficient, working class, County Durham mining village with several well stocked shops and businesses providing for people's everyday needs.

John Young's Post Office in High Street provided a telephone and telegraph service together with two daily postal collections and deliveries, with letters collected from boxes in the village and surrounding areas at Greenhead, Low Beechburn, Valley Terrace, Victoria and North Bitchburn. This, together with the North Eastern Railway from Beechburn Station, were vital links with the wider world and proved invaluable during the war years for families eager to exchange news with their loved ones serving in the armed forces. Sadly, the news was not always good.

THE STATION AND STATION ROAD, HOWDEN-LE-WEAR

The railway station at Beechburn for Howden-le-Wear.   Lines led towards Crook up a steep gradient through a deep cutting. The footbridge is now part of Rowley Station at Beamish Museum. The large building on the right is Craig Hall, formerly Blue Parrot Club, British Workmen's Hall and Cinema. Bridge Street is in the background

Image courtesy of Howden-le-Wear History Society

According to the 1914 Kelly's Directory of Durham, village shops included a baker, three butchers, a branch of Crook Co-operative Society, two drapers, newsagent, two hairdressers, boot repairer, confectioner, fishmonger, two grocers, two general dealer shopkeepers, ironmonger, undertaker with joiner's workshop and two blacksmiths' forges.

Public Houses were in abundance: The Plantation Inn, Australian Hotel, Green Tree Inn, Surtees Hotel at Valley Terrace; at Fir Tree, the Duke of York and Fir Tree Inn; at Hargill, the Grey Horse and Hargill Inn; and the Colliery Inn at Low Beechburn.

To counteract the workers' indulgence in alcoholic beverage, the Rechabites held regular meetings at the Methodist Chapels, advocating teetotal abstinence. To be fair, not everyone frequented licensed premises, and many family lives revolved round the two Methodist Chapels, Wesleyans in High Street and Primitives in Bridge Street, or St Mary's Church of England where, together with their Sunday Schools, a wide range of associated activities took place throughout the week as well as on Sundays.

The British Workmen's Hall in Station Road provided a lecture room, news and recreational rooms and a library containing 250 volumes. As not everyone had access to newspapers, this establishment played an important role in disseminating current news and information.

The Women's Institute was established in Howden-le-Wear in November 1916 with Mrs Fryer of Smelt House as the first President. Meetings were held in the church schoolroom or in the British Workmen's Hall, before a purpose built hall was opened in November 1925 with seating for 250 people, a tea room, kitchen and offices. The hall became a central resource for Howden-le-Wear hosting WI meetings, wedding receptions, dances and concerts.

Most of the land round Howden-le-Wear was owned by Chaytors, Shaftoes, Coal Companies or was part of the Smelt House Estate. Consequently farms were operated by tenant farmers producing food for local consumption, fresh milk delivered daily from the dairy by milk float, butter, cheese, eggs, potatoes and turnips. Animals were slaughtered locally in the village behind Balmer's butcher's shop, producing pork, bacon, ham, beef, lamb, mutton and chicken. There were also a few orchards attached to farms and bigger houses providing fruits in season, and many people foraged in the countryside for the natural harvest it provided. Miners in particular made the most of their leisure time, spending much of it outdoors in the fresh air, tending large vegetable gardens or allotments, while some reared chickens, hens or rabbits to supplement the family diet.

It must be remembered that housing conditions in Howden-le-Wear were not particularly good in 1914. There was no electricity or mains gas supply to the village and so oil lamps and candles were still being used for lighting. Streets and the railway station were still dimly illuminated by paraffin oil lamps. Victorian inventions and improvements were beginning to be more widely adopted, with the more affluent homes affording things like treadle sewing machines and patent carpet sweepers which were not nearly as effective as taking the proddy mats outside and giving them a good beating. Many working class dwellings still had no bathrooms, so the tin bath in front of the living room fire remained in use with hot water from the coal fired range and cold water from a communal tap in the yard or scullery basin. Cooking was done in the oven or in pans on the same open coal fire.

Most toilets were outside, 'down the garden' or 'across the yard' where the ash closet was situated. By 1914, Howden-le-Wear streets had been linked into the main Crook sewer which followed the route of the Beechburn Beck and some of the larger houses were connected to main drains and so had the old ash closets converted to water closets with a flushing system, but the majority relied upon the weekly scavenger man from the council to clean out the 'netties'. Chamber pots were in common use for 'overnight calls of nature'.

Monday was traditionally 'washing day' when the family washing was done in a poss tub and wrung out through the mangle. A few people had Victorian hand operated washing machines, but even these were hard work. On dry days, clothes were then hung out to dry on clothes lines propped up across the streets. If the weather was wet, the damp clothes were placed on a wooden clothes horse in front of the kitchen fire. Once dry, the clothes were ironed using flat irons heated in the fire.

The fireplace and kitchen table were the central features of every living room as so many domestic activities took place there. Nowadays the television, mobile phones or the computer are the centre of attention in many rooms.

Despite the lack of modern domestic facilities, housewives, in the main, were proud of their homes and kept them as comfortable, clean and tidy as possible. Most families existed according to a familiar weekly routine in step with the weather and seasons of the year.

There were very few cars or other forms of motor transport, horses still providing the power to move carts and carriages. A few people had bicycles, but not many in the village could afford one.

Old Church Street at the turn of the 20th century.

Image courtesy of Howden-le-Wear History Society

A steam roller repairing the roads.

Image courtesy of Howden-le-Wear History Society

Roads were not well surfaced and, although maintained by the local council steam roller, many remained little more than cart tracks of compacted stones and earth with frequent pot holes and ruts.

The railway transported goods and people long distances, but horses took over from the stations to the destinations. People walked to visit locally or took the train to Crook or Bishop Auckland.

A number of shopkeepers and businesses, farmers, the Co-op, greengrocer, fishmonger, oil-man, coal-man, grocer etc. also had horse drawn carts to deliver goods to their customers. Every day some local trader would be round the streets with a horse and cart, selling door to door – a valuable service to the housewives, but woe betide any that interfered with the washing lines. The 'scouring stone' man or 'rag and bone' man was also a regular visitor, collecting old rags, bones and scrap metal items in exchange for a scouring stone which was used to rub clean the front door step – the pride of every housewife. This was recycling 100 years ago.

In 1914 there was a vibrant community spirit in Howden-le-Wear with people eager to take part in a variety of organised activities. There was rarely a time when there would not be a dance to look forward to, concert or performance to rehearse, or meeting to attend. Visiting the local pub, chapel, church, workmen's hall or other organisation was probably a welcome means of escape from the overcrowded living conditions large families found themselves in.

A newspaper report in the Durham and County Chronicle dated Thursday, 6th July 1916 recorded village ladies supporting the war effort:

> *'Howden-le-Wear was not behindhand on Saturday in its endeavour to do its 'bit' for the 6th D.L.I. in aid of which, a Flag Day was held. The heavy rain somewhat marred the proceedings but despite this the young ladies were diligent, and took special care that no-one was missed.'*

❖ *EMPLOYMENT &*
WORKING CONDITIONS

In 1914, the majority of men from Howden-le-Wear and district were employed in coal mining and associated industries of coke production, brickyards and pipes. In this area, many small coal pits were in operation employing men and boys from the village and surrounding region.

One of the largest complexes was at North Bitchburn where the North Bitchburn Coal Company employed 298 men, 229 underground and 69 on the surface.   Coal was mined from the Ballarat, Brockwell, (main seam of good coal 4 ft 6 in thick with an adjacent 2 ft seam of seggar/fireclay), Constantine, Five Quarter, Harvey, Top Main and Victoria seams. The manager, James Widdas Pescod, under-manager, George French, and agent, Thomas Heslop, were in charge. This complex of drift mines, coke ovens and fireclay brick and pipe making kilns, situated at the end of Valley Terrace below North Beechburn, finally closed in 1966.

Miners at the entrance to drift mine, most probably Hargill Colliery.
Image courtesy of Howden-le-Wear History Society

In 1914, Hargill Hill Colliery employed 9 men, 5 underground and 4 above. They worked the main coal seam only 29 ft below the surface and the Brockwell 6 ft thick with good fireclay 1 ft 6 in thick adjacent. The coal was sold for household use and manufacturing. Esther Lowson was manager and J.H. Dent under-manager. Following a disastrous fire one Sunday morning the mine was abandoned and closed in 1934.

Thistleflat Colliery (Low Beechburn) owned by Low Beechburn Coal Company Ltd. produced coal for coking and manufacture together with fireclay for the local brickyard. In 1914,136 men and boys, 104 underground and 32 above, worked the Busty, Harvey, Hutton and Yard seams. The manager, Robert Robson, was well qualified with 1st class certificates in Mine Management and Surveying. He went on to manage other coal mines in the area. The workings at Thistleflat were finally abandoned in 1937.

Bridgefield House, home of Mr Brackenbury who owned Rumby Hill Colliery.

Image courtesy of Howden-le-Wear History Society

John Henry Brackenbury, who lived in Bridgefield House, Howden-le-Wear, owned Rumby Hill Colliery. In 1914, he employed only 10 men, 8 below and 2 above ground. They worked the Ballarat seam for household coal and manufacturing. After exhausting the workable reserves the Colliery finally closed in 1944.

At Marshall Green Colliery in 1914, Wear Valley Coal & Brick Co. employed 34 men, 30 underground and 4 surface workers, where they worked the Ganister seam for fireclay and Marshall Green seam for coal. The fireclay was processed and fired in coal fired kilns producing bricks and pipes. The colliery closed in 1955.

There were numerous coal pits in the vicinity of Howden-le-Wear, especially around Crook at Woodifield, Wooley, White Lea and the large Peases West Complex at Billy Row and Roddymoor. Others were at Witton-le-Wear, Fir Tree and Harperley where seams were near the surface.

Group of workers at the Pipeworks, 1900.

Image courtesy of Howden-le-Wear History Society

Work in these coal mines was hard and dangerous with a high accident rate, frequently fatal. Most common incidents involved falls of stone or machinery accidents such as being run over by moving tubs or faulty equipment. Many pitmen suffered ill health brought on by the dark, heavy, underground working conditions where the atmosphere was highly polluted with coal dust and stythe, and frequently wet, waterlogged and cramped. They were not well paid and, with no long-term contracts of employment, frequently moved about between mines seeking the best deal.

At West Bitchburn Colliery, Howden-le-Wear, the West Beechburn Coal and Whinstone Co. Ltd. employed 76 men and boys, 64 under and 12 above ground, to mine coal from the Victoria Seam. On 22nd January 1918, Thomas Pearson, an 18 year old driver, was killed by a fall of stone. His weekly wage was £1 8s 6d. The Durham Miners' Association Compensation Committee agreed upon £50 as a settlement payment to his family.

Miners' banner of West Beechburn Colliery. The pit was destroyed by a spectacular fire one Sunday afternoon in 1926 which led to the colliery being abandoned.

Image courtesy of Howden-le-Wear History Society

The numerous brickyards and pipe works provided further employment, as did the railways and farms, but manual labour was not well paid and large families often struggled financially. It was from working conditions such as these that many men were recruited to the armed forces where pay was assured.

From 1910 to 1914, Britain was racked by a series of strikes that were noted for workers' refusal to follow the dictates of union leaders. This shook the British capitalist state to its foundations and forced the Liberal government of Asquith to turn to military means to keep order. Up to 1910, coal mining in County Durham was an apparent booming industry with miners enjoying an unprecedented period of prosperity.

Workforce at the local pipe works. Coal fired kilns produced pipes, drainage equipment, junctions, bends and even garden jardinières, all with the familiar golden brown salt glaze.

Image courtesy of Howden-le-Wear History Society

Highest paid were experienced hewers receiving up to 17s 10d per shift depending on output and the current price of coal. However, most workers were paid under 4 shillings a day basic pay. High wages attracted men to the industry but unfortunately, for a variety of reasons, productivity declined and the position of Durham miners was becoming increasingly precarious. The small drift mines around Howden-le-Wear were becoming increasingly difficult to work profitably owing to worked-out seams and, unlike larger collieries where investment in electrification and mechanisation was affordable, relatively primitive methods, with dated machinery, were still being used in the wet and poorly ventilated adits.

During the parliament of 1911, far reaching schemes of social insurance were introduced and carried by law. The scheme was in two parts, the first relating to Health Insurance and the second to Unemployment Insurance, but the Durham Association of Mine Workers and Mechanics decided not to take part in the administration of the Act. This decision left the members free to take up membership of any Friendly Society they chose. The second part of the Act, relating to unemployment ,did not apply to colliery workers.

Wages had remained static whilst prices had increased and, in an attempt to stimulate the economy, the capitalist mine owners cut wages even further and expected the men to work harder to increase productivity. Tension was slowly building between workers and employers. The unrest spread quickly as many railway workers also took strike action and, in some places, troops were deployed to quell local unrest.

Local coal miners. They are resting on their hunkers, a familiar seating position of pitmen, probably reflecting the confines of their workplace. The Deputy is the man with the stick in the centre. Note the 'midgie lamp' with the next man. Naked flames were considered safe in the shallow mines of this area.

Image courtesy of Howden-le-Wear History Society

Miners' minimum wage had only recently been legislated after the 1912 strikes, but part of the workmen's wages was a coal allowance and free colliery house, although not all workers were entitled to these benefits. Usually only the married men at the top of the wage scale received a colliery cottage. The coal owners did not operate their pits every day – often closing them when prices dropped – so the men were never sure whether they were working or not. Since wages were tied to the number of days worked and output, idle pits meant a loss of family income. If a stoppage lasted for any length of time the miners moved on to another colliery in the hope of finding work.

There was comparatively little employment for women who, in many families, stayed at home looking after numerous children. Because of this mobile workforce, single men were often found lodging with relatives or other families.

Denebridge in Howden-le-Wear.

Image courtesy of Howden-le-Wear History Society

There was no official welfare relief, other than the Poor Law, so the consequences of a man sustaining injury or dying were very great indeed. Relief funds were set up to assist in some cases but were of limited help, especially where a family was expected to vacate its colliery owned house when the main breadwinner was incapacitated or died. Men were encouraged to contribute to 'Friendly Societies' which paid out some money in times of hardship.

Some union associations tried to improve workers' pay and conditions, but mine owners actively discouraged membership and fined members for showing allegiance. Very little heed was taken of the 'Health & Safety' of the workmen who were expected to take care of themselves in very dangerous and difficult conditions. Consequently, accident and death rates were high.

The outbreak of war in 1914 seemed to cover up the flaws for a further five years as people united against a common enemy. However, the first effect of the war was the dislocation of trade, and this dislocation reflected itself in the working of the collieries, where short time became very prevalent and for at least six months very few days were worked. By the beginning of 1915, it was evident that some change would have to be made in wages as the price of goods necessary for life was soaring rapidly. In Durham, four different societies, the Association of Miners, the Association of Cokemen, the Association of Enginemen and the Association of Mechanics, at first could not agree as all had different pay scales for the different jobs. They eventually combined to form the Miners' Federation whose representatives agreed to meet the mine owners and, on 11th May 1915, a final offer of 15% on basic rates was accepted.

As the war progressed, the government found it necessary to take charge of the coal industry in the national interests and a 'Coal Controller' was appointed as Chief Officer in February 1917. This made a tremendous difference as far as wage regulation was concerned. Instead of wages being regulated locally they began to be determined on a national basis, and from that time the Miners' Federation became responsible for all wage negotiations. In September 1917, an increase of 1s 6d per day to those over 16 years of age and 9 pence per day to those under 16 years old was given, being known as the 'War Wage'. This was a flat rate increase awarded across all classes of work and the following year, in June 1918, a similar increase was awarded with the same conditions applying.

With the continuance of the war, workmen were requested to allow demands for improvement of their working conditions to lie in abeyance and this request was honoured. There was, however, growing discontent over a number of underlying concerns regarding working hours – the miners wanted a 48 hour week, and wage regulation. In order to strengthen their position, the Durham Miners' Association and Colliery Mechanics' Association voted on 17th August 1918 to become affiliated to the Miners' Federation.

With the end of wartime strain, pent up feelings seemed to lose all restraint and the vexed question of working hours led to immediate conflict with the mine owners and some tough negotiation. The war having ended, mineworkers felt that an improvement in their working conditions with greater remuneration was long overdue. Furthermore, following the demobilisation of troops and the large numbers of men seeking to return to employment, it was expected that measures would be taken to alleviate this situation. The Durham Miners' Federation suggested that reducing the working day would create more vacancies for returning miners. In 1919, the government, by Royal Commission, instigated an enquiry, presided over by Mr Justice Sankey, to investigate miners' grievances. On 20th March 1919, three reports were presented to the government, the Majority Report, the Sankey Report and the Coal Owners' Report. The government announced its decision to adopt the Sankey Report, thus forming a basis for mine workers' terms of employment for many years to come.

❖ *WWI 1914 - 1915*

The Great War was a major turning point in the history of the 20th Century. The assassination of the heir to the Austro-Hungarian throne, Archduke Ferdinand and his wife, on the 28th June 1914 was the catalyst that led the world into the decline that made war inevitable. Two opposing alliances were formed – the Allies (Britain, France and Russia) and the Central Powers (Germany, Austro-Hungry and the Ottoman Empire).

Following Germany's invasion of Belgium on the 3rd August 1914, Great Britain declared war on Germany, and many of the Commonwealth powers quickly aligned themselves with the Allies. There is no accurate record of the number of lives lost, but the approximate numbers are as follows:

Allies	Killed	Central Powers	Killed
Britain and Empire	958,000	Germany	1,800,000
France and colonies	1,400,000	Austro-Hungarian Empire	1,200,000
Russia	1,700,000	Turkey	325,000
Italy	650,000	Bulgaria	87,000
Romania	335,000		
USA	116,000		
Serbia	48,000		
Belgium	14,000		
Portugal	7,000		
Greece	5,000		
Japan	300		

August 1914 saw the first contingent of the British Expeditionary Force leave UK shores for France and by the 23rd of the month they were engaged with the enemy in the Battle of Mons. The Battle of the Marne halted the German advance to Paris and the race to the French northern coast began. In September, the Battle of the Aisne marked the start of trench warfare which was to continue for four years, and in October the first of three battles began for the strategic town of Ypres. This marked the beginning of a conflict which changed the lives of many, including the families of the soldiers back home in Howden-le-Wear and Fir Tree.

In 1915 the use of poison gas was experienced by troops on both sides and became one of the most feared weapons. Crude gas masks were distributed to soldiers and early gases were designed to be more of an irritant than a killer. Chlorine gas was first used in the Second Battle of Ypres in 1915 which caused horrific injuries on both sides. Phosgene and mustard gases were later used with devastating effect to internal organs and in many cases caused permanent blindness. Many thousands of men survived the war but were so badly incapacitated by gas that they could not work when they returned to civilian life.

The Gallipoli Campaign began and finished in 1915 with a major defeat for the allied armies. Fighting was taking place not only in France and Flanders, but in Salonika and Egypt. Soldiers were fighting from all over the world, including Australia, New Zealand and Africa, as well as from many of the German colonies.

It truly was becoming a global war.

❖ *1915*

The men from Howden-le-Wear who lost their lives during this year were:

Joseph Nutley, Charles Hindmoor, **Sydney Hardy, George Clark** and **Thomas Brett**.

Joseph Nutley

James Nutley and Eleanor Jolley were married in 1872 and Joseph was one of their thirteen children. The family first appeared on the 1881 Census, at Constantine Farm at Quarry Burn, by which time they had five children, two of whom were at school.

James, originally from Whitehaven, was a coal miner and, like so many, worked in the same industry for decades. Ten years later they were living in Railway Street and had ten children at home. Two sons were coal miners and a third, aged fourteen, was a school teacher. Joseph was now three years old.

In 1901 and living at a Hargill Road address, father James had risen to deputy at the mine and Joseph was a grocer's apprentice at fourteen years of age.

James Nutley, Joseph's father, in later years.
Image courtesy of Nutley Family

In the last Census that can be accessed, that of 1911, Joseph had left the family home and the grocery trade and was to be found in Horden, boarding with the Rose family. He was now working underground as a labourer. What a difference four years make.

It is known that Joseph served in the Northumberland Fusiliers,"B" Company of the 2nd Battalion, and a photograph shows him clad in a light coloured uniform, which was commonly issued for use in tropical climates. It is most likely that he enlisted prior to August 1914 and was a regular soldier. In 1914, the battalion had been based in India and Joseph most likely saw service there. In December they returned to England, and joined the 84th Brigade, 28th Division.

Joseph Nutley and his eldest brother Thomas. There was a fifteen year age difference. Joseph is in tropical uniform and was on leave from serving with the Northumberland Fusiliers in India prior to the outbreak of WWI.
Image courtesy of the Nutley Family

"The Long, Long Trail" describes how they were: *"..... rushed in as a much needed reinforcement to France"*. The units of the division embarked at Southampton and landed at Le Havre on January 16th - 19th 1915 and then moved to the area between Bailleul and Hazebrouck. This information tallies with the date on Joseph's WWI Medal Roll Card which states that he went on overseas service on 16th January 1915.

17

Joseph was in Flanders for only a short while and was lost on the 21st February. 'Lost' is a small but important word as, in March 1915, the Newcastle Journal listed a great many soldiers from the Northumberland Fusiliers who had been wounded and included the names of twenty five men who were missing, one of whom was Joseph Nutley.

His Medal Roll Card shows "presumed dead" and his name on the Ypres (Menin Gate) Memorial was placed on a supplementary panel. There was great confusion over the names to go on the memorials and it appears that Private J Nutley's name was not on the initial engraving of the panel for the Northumberland Fusiliers. This was a common problem and, once the panels had been engraved, they could not be changed. Addenda panels were added to include men who were declared missing from a variety of regiments including Joseph Nutley whose name appears on Panel 58.

NICHOLLS C.
          KING'S SHROPSHIRE L. I.
NICHOLLS J. W. YORKSHIRE REGIMENT
NUTLEY J. NORTHUMBERLAND FUSILIERS
OLIVER J. H EAST YORKSHIRE REGIMENT
OSBORNE A.   ROYAL FUSILIERS

Joseph Nutley's name on Panel 58 on the Menin Gate Memorial at Ypres.
Image courtesy of the Nutley Family

Whatever his precise fate, the fact remains that Private 3408 Nutley never made it home again to Howden-le-Wear. Joseph Nutley is one of 54,631 men commemorated on the Ypres Menin Gate Memorial and is also remembered in a brief sentence on the headstone of his parents' grave in St. Mary's churchyard, Howden-le-Wear.

Transcription: *'In memory of James Nutley who died November 11th 1927 aged 75 years. Also Eleanor his beloved wife who died January 6th 1929 aged 74 years. Also Private Joseph Nutley, N.F. their son, who died at Ypres   February 21st 1915 aged 28 years.*
"At rest"'

In addition, a processional cross was commissioned which was held within St. Mary's Church, Howden-le-Wear. The inscription reads:

'In loving memory of Joseph Nutley, 2nd N.F. who fell in
the Great War at Ypres on February 21st 1915.

This cross is given by his brother George Nutley'.

When the Church was deconsecrated in 2008 the cross was returned to the family.

Charles William Hindmoor

Charles William Hindmoor was born in Tow Law in County Durham in 1878. His father, Charles Hindmoor, was born in Evenwood in County Durham in 1838, and was a joiner. His mother, Hannah Gray, was born in Sunderland in 1847 and lived until 1925. The Census of 1881 shows the family living in Front Street, Howden-le-Wear. Charles William had an older sister, Mary Ann, born in 1875, also born in Tow Law, who later married George Cummings in 1896.

At the time of the 1891 Census the family is now living in High Street, Howden-le-Wear. Charles Hindmoor, the father, is still a carpenter and joiner, and Charles William, now aged 13, is a coal miner. He has two further brothers, George, born in 1881 and who died in 1894, and Richard, born in 1884 and who died in 1957. In 1908 Richard married Elizabeth Calvert.

By 1901 the family is living at Stable Row, Howden-le-Wear. The Census shows that the occupation of Charles Hindmoor, the father, is still a colliery carpenter and joiner, while the occupation of Charles William, now aged 23, is shown as a colliery hewer. Charles William's younger brother Richard, now aged 16, is also a coal miner.

By the time of the 1911 Census, the family has moved yet again, and is now living in The Square, Howden-le-Wear. The Census shows the occupation of Charles Hindmoor senior, now aged 73, as a colliery joiner, but he is shown as out of work. Charles William, now aged 33, still single and living with his parents, is also shown as a coal miner hewer, but he too is shown as being out of work. He was now, however, a Special Reservist in the Durham Light Infantry.

Private Charles Hindmoor of the 2nd Durham Light Infantry. *Image courtesy of the Auckland Chronicle 9.5.1915*

The first fragment of his enlistment form shows his age as 32 years 6 months. The birth records show the registration of a Charles William Hindmoor in the first quarter of 1878 in the district of Weardale. This would place his enlistment in mid-1910. He was placed in the 3rd Battalion, DLI. This was a Reserve Battalion, as the first fragment of his enlistment form shows, classing him as a Special Reservist. The Special Reserve, which was introduced in 1908, was a way of building up a body of trained reservists in addition to the soldiers of the regular Army Reserve. This Special Reserve provided a form of part-time military service. Its members enlisted for a period of 6 years, and had to accept the possibility of their being called up should there be a general mobilisation, and they had to accept all the same conditions as the men in the Army Reserve. In one major respect the Special Reserve differed from the Territorial Force in that its members could be sent overseas. On becoming a Special Reservist, a soldier started with six months' full-time preliminary training, with the same pay as a regular, and then had to do 3 to 4 weeks' training per year after that.

The second fragment of his enlistment form shows that he re-enlisted, and states that his *"Service towards engagement reckons from 31st August 1914"*. We see that on three different occasions he was absent, and for the first of these absences was punished by the forfeit of his pay. Now that he was in the army as a full-time soldier, he was posted to the Expeditionary Force with the 2nd Battalion, DLI.

In the summer of 1914, the reservists were based at Lichfield. As the orders for mobilisation were refined, the men were medically examined as they arrived, and, on being passed fit, were issued with their kit, all the necessary equipment being in place to help make the process smooth and efficient. Nominal rolls were filled in, and the men were prepared for despatch to the 2nd Battalion, DLI. It is interesting to note that the officers at the depot recorded that almost all the regular reservists reported sober and on time, whereas those of the Special Reserve, i.e. the 3rd and 4th Battalions, were mainly late and many were under the influence of alcohol. As a result, many had to follow on behind the main party after it was deployed.

On the 7th August 1914 the battalion paraded ready to move to Dunfermline for further training. Here, as a result of so many reservists having been recalled to the colours, route marching and the breaking in of new boots became a priority.

In France, meanwhile, the first five divisions of the British Expeditionary Force had been in action against the Germans at Mons in Belgium, and had started to fall back towards Le Cateau. It was now that the 6th Division, which incorporated Charles William Hindmoor's battalion, was ordered to assemble, and the various units began to move to the divisional assembly area. As a result, the 2nd Battalion, DLI, moved from Dunfermline bound for Southampton where they boarded two ships sailing for St Nazaire, landing on 10th September.

The battalion moved to a rest camp, but were there for only one night when they were ordered to board a train to the front. Here, on the 19th September, for the first time in France, the battalion took over the front line. The division arrived in time to reinforce the hard-pressed British Expeditionary Force, before the whole army was moved north into Flanders, and remained on the Western Front throughout the war.

Over the following months the battalion was involved in various battles, including the Battle of the Aisne, which marked the beginning of trench warfare, but mainly in a defensive role. Although there were quiet periods, there were also huge-scale savage battles, and the fighting on the Western Front never stopped. At this time, constant shelling and deadly sniping claimed many casualties, and the terrible winter weather caused problems with the flimsy parapets of the trenches.

On the early evening of the 6th May, 1915, the 2nd Battalion moved back into the front near Le Touquet. In this sector the battalion held a stretch of trench 900 yards long, parts of which were only 25 yards from the trenches held by the Germans. The British trenches were much poorer than those previously held, and a great deal of energy was spent trying to improve them. Mining operations were carried out in the battalion's sector in an effort to plant mines under the enemy trenches and blow up their front-line positions. Another novelty was the use of catapults to throw bombs over to the enemy, and early trench mortars were making their appearance.

On the 16th May the battalion commenced their next tour of the line in the Le Touquet sector. Here they remained for eight days, and it was during this tour, on the 21st May 1915, at the age of 37, that Charles William Hindmoor was killed in action and was buried in Strand Military Cemetery.

His will, a very brief document written in his own hand, states that he left all his property to his parents:

Charles Hindmoor's will which was hand written prior to front line service. All servicemen made a will which was included in their records. They often had a personal copy in their pay book.

Image courtesy of Howden-le-Wear History Society

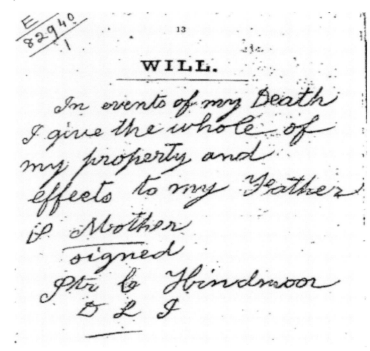

Private Charles Hindmoor's statement of service. It shows he enlisted on the 31st August 1914. He had several conduct issues when he was 'absent without leave 'and for one period of 6 days for which he forfeited 6 days' pay. The record is one of the 'burnt records' which survived the London Blitz in 1940. Only 40% of all records still exist.

Image courtesy of www. ancestry.co.uk

The Medal Roll Card of Private Charles Hindmoor.

Each serviceman had one and it shows his regimental number 10194 and that he served with the DLI. The qualifying date at the bottom identifies when he went into a war zone and above it states it was France. The card shows he was eligible for the Victory Medal, the British Medal and the 1915 Star. It also states that he died in service.

Image courtesy of
www.ancestry.co.uk

Sydney Hardy

Sydney Hardy was born in the summer of 1893 in Howden-le-Wear. In 1901 the family was living in Church Street and by 1911 they were living at Loves Beechburn. His father was William Hardy, born in Newfield, County Durham, c1861 and his mother was Sarah Pattison, also born c1861, but in Hanley, Staffordshire. They were married in 1883 and had 8 children: Wilfred, Marion, Blanche, Sydney, Roy, Alan, Myra and another who died. Also living with the family in 1911 was Wilhelmina Hardy, William's and Sarah's 3 year old granddaughter born at the end of 1907, who was possibly Blanche's daughter.

In 1911, Sydney and his brother Roy were coal mining putters, and father William and brother Wilfred were coal mining hewers.

Wilfred volunteered and enlisted in the Royal Engineers (102877) and Sydney enlisted in the Northumberland Fusiliers. The Northumberland Fusiliers were known as the "Fighting Fifth" as the regiment was until 1881 the Fifth Foot, and the Northumberland Fusiliers raised no fewer than 51 battalions for service in the Great War. This makes it the second largest after the London Regiment.

53. THE "FIGHTING FIFTH" (NORTHUMBERLAND FUSILIERS) AFTER THE BATTLE OF ST. ELOI.

**The Fighting Fifth (Northumberland Fusiliers) after the Battle of St Eloi.
Here Lance Corporal Sydney Hardy fought during April 1915.**
Image courtesy of Anne Yuill

1st Northumberland Fusiliers was part of 9th Brigade based in Portsmouth, and the 3rd Division. They had landed at Le Havre on 14th August 1914 and Sydney was transported to France on the 28th November 1914. They saw heavy fighting through the winter including St Eloi in April. It appears Sydney was a good soldier and he was promoted to lance corporal in the field.

The Commonwealth War Graves Certificate states that Sydney died on the 7th July 1915. The war diaries for the battalion show that they were on training duties all through July, but they were involved in very heavy fighting in the previous month. The Medal Roll Card and the Soldiers of the Great War database show he died of his wounds. His body was never found and he is remembered on the memorial in Harlebeke New British Cemetery, 32 miles east of Ypres. If Sydney died of wounds presumably in a clearing station or front line hospital, then he would have had a known grave. It is therefore reasonable to assume that Sydney was fighting with the Northumberland Fusiliers and during the battle near Bellewarde Farm on the 16th/17th June he was one of the many men who were declared missing. Casualties were very high on both sides and the Northumberland Fusiliers experienced fierce shell and artillery bombardment, gas shells and ferocious hand to hand fighting in the German trenches. They reached the third line of German trenches before being repulsed and they had to move back to their original position. On the 18th June, Brigadier General Douglas Smith visited the men left in the front line to express his appreciation of the good work done by the battalion during the operations on the 16th June.

Private Sydney Hardy is remembered on the Howden-le-Wear War Memorial but is listed as a Private and not as a Lance Corporal. His brother Wilfred survived the war and was living at The Hollow in Crook. There is no evidence to indicate that any of his other brothers served in the armed forces during the war.

George Clark

A tactic employed by both sides of WWI was that of tunnelling under enemy lines to place and detonate explosive charges. Hill 60 was located about 3 miles south east of Ypres in Flanders. It was not a natural feature but was built up from spoil removed during the construction of a nearby railway cutting. It was 60 metres above sea level – hence Hill 60 – and because it was elevated land, it was of great strategic importance to whoever held it during the battles of the Salient.

Following fierce fighting, sometimes by poisonous gas attack, the Hill changed hands between the Germans and Allies several times. Whilst the Germans had control, the allies made continued attempts to undermine the area and plant explosives to detonate and destroy the enemy forces. Four tunnels known as M1, M2, M3 & M3A were dug and mines detonated in 1914.

Deep mining continued under the German galleries in late August 1915 with 175th Tunnelling Company digging a gallery 220 yds (200m) behind the British front line and passing 90 ft (27m) beneath. The 3rd Canadian Tunnelling Company took over in April/May of 1916 and completed the galleries, charged the tunnels with 53,300 lbs (24,000 kg) of explosives in July 1916, and a branch gallery under the Caterpillar was filled with 70,000 lbs (32,000 kg) in October.

In November 1916, the 1st Australian Tunnelling Company took over and maintained the tunnels until, at 3.10am on June 7th 1917, 19 mines totalling 450,000 kg (990,000 lbs) were detonated under German lines. The blast created one of the largest non-nuclear explosions in history, reportedly heard in London and Dublin. It killed 10,000 German soldiers.

Countless soldiers toiled in the cold, dark tunnels: many died there and were buried in the clay.   Hill 60 is now preserved as an official War Grave.

Hill 60 as it is today with some live ammunition which still lies on the ground. *Image courtesy of William Clark*

When local people at Howden-le-Wear heard about the Hill 60 exploits they nicknamed some old coal-mine workings and spoil heaps on Constantine Hillside 'Hill 60' and it became a popular place for village children to explore and play. The remains of the old workings can be seen today above Jubilee Park and it is still referred to as Hill 60.

Following the outbreak of war in 1914, both sides soon realised that tunnelling under enemy lines could be effective, and this meant that the allies were constantly on the lookout for experienced tunnellers. North East England was a prime recruitment area as Durham coalminers proved to be excellent sappers for this dangerous work. Men were recruited from the many pits around Howden-le-Wear and in 1914, following a recruitment drive at Beechburn Colliery, George Clark, a 40 year old coal miner from Howden-le-Wear, enlisted at London.

George Clark in the centre with the ball whilst playing for the Howden-le-Wear AFC. *Image courtesy of William Clark*

George was married to wife Amelia and they lived in a two roomed back to back house in High Street with their young family of six sons and two daughters. He was a keen sportsman and played football for Howden-le-Wear Association Football Club. In 1897/98 season they won the Northern League, H Division title.

George Clarke.
Image courtesy of William Clark

George and Amelia had a large family. Their first born was Robert Taylor in 1899, followed in 1901 by William, and then on 4th July 1903 they had a daughter, Irene. On 12th October 1905 another daughter, Edna, was born. Another son, Lenneth, was born on 26th April 1908. George junior was born on 24th April 1910, Edgar on 15th October 1912 and finally Colin on 30th July 1914. Colin was only 18 months old when his father was killed.

All 10 of them lived in a small two bedroomed back to back house in High Street before moving to a similar terrace house at 18, Victoria Row.

According to the Admission Register, the children all attended Howden-le-Wear school. When living at High Street, George admitted Irene to the Mixed School on the 15th August 1910, but together with the whole class, she was returned to the Infant School for a further year until re-admitted to the Mixed School on the 14th August 1911. He admitted Edna to Infants on the 17th October 1910 and to the Mixed School on the 19th August 1912, and Lenneth enrolled on the 19th May 1913. While on leave from the army, George Junior was the last member of the family whom George was to register at school on the 3rd May 1915.

Working as a hewer at Beechburn Colliery would not be well paid and perhaps the prospect of earning more money for his family helped George decide to enlist at his age. Little would he realise that a few years later his eldest son would also be involved in the conflict.

George enlisted in the Royal Engineers as Sapper Number 112627 and was quickly attached to the 175th Tunnelling Company. This company was formed at Terdeghem in April 1915, and moved soon after into the Railway Wood, Hooge, Armagh Wood areas of the Ypres Salient. They extended to Hill 60 in July 1915 before being relieved in May 1916 by the 1st Australian Tunnelling Company.

Unfortunately, whilst working above ground, on 11th December 1915 George was killed in action by enemy fire and has no known grave. He was killed somewhere in the Ypres Salient, and no other members of the tunnelling company were killed in the weeks on either side of the 11th December 1915.

His widow Amelia, who was now living with the family in 18 Victoria Row, Howden-le-Wear, was notified of her husband's death and an obituary was published in the *Auckland Chronicle*.

George is remembered on the Menin Gate in Ypres and his name was added to the memorial in Howden-le-Wear.

George would never know that his eldest son Robert Taylor Clark would also be a casualty of the same conflict. What a sad house there must have been in Victoria Row when peace was declared in 1918, where Amelia was bereft of both husband and eldest son.

Menin Gate Memorial in Ypres.
Image courtesy of William Clark

Thomas Brett

Thomas Brett has been a difficult man to identify. On the War Memorial in Howden-le-Wear, the name G. Brett, Sapper with the Royal Engineers, is named. When researching the CWGC database there is no G. Brett listed who died with the Royal Engineers. There are, however, 6 men with the surname Brett who served with the Royal Engineers and lost their lives. Sapper Arthur Brett came from Hull, Sapper John Brett came from London, Corporal William Brett was buried in his home town of Mitcham, and Sergeant J. Brett came from London. It is reasonable to assume that they can be discounted.

That left two Sappers, Thomas Brett who served with the Inland Water Transport and who died 24th October 1918 and was buried in Longuenesse (St Omer) Souvenir Cemetery in France. There is no Thomas Brett on the Absent Voters' List that was compiled prior to October 1918, which means that this man was less likely to be the Howden-le-Wear casualty.

The final soldier was Thomas Brett who served in the Royal Engineers with the 178th Tunnelling Company and had the number 112628. He was the brother of James Brett who lived at 66 Fourth Street, West Stanley, in County Durham. Thomas died on the 21st December 1915 and is remembered on the Menin Gate in Ypres. This is most likely to be the soldier named on the Howden-le-Wear War Memorial.

There are two possible Brett families to which he could have belonged. There was a Thomas born in Bishop Auckland in 1871 and he had a brother James four years younger. The family moved to Crook and then to Coundon. His father came from Ireland and was a miner. For some unknown reason, Thomas is difficult to find in any further Census. He was 45 years old when he died, which would fit with this Thomas.

The other family lived at Billy Row, Crook, and this Thomas was born around 1880 and had a brother James three years older. This was also a family of coal miners. In 1911, this Thomas was living at 16 Institute Terrace, Crook. Thomas's age would mean that he was 35 when he died, and not 45 as stated on the CWGC database. This could be a possible error.

Coming from mining stock it is plausible that, whichever Thomas it was, he became a miner, which would fit into serving with the Tunnelling Companies of the Royal Engineers, as Durham miners had the reputation as the best people to have in these regiments.

Thomas Brett's Medal Roll Card shows he served with the Royal Engineers and that he was Killed in Action on 21st December 1915, just over three weeks after arriving in France. *Image courtesy of www.ancestry.co.uk*

❖ *1916*

1916 saw the war of attrition continue on the Western Front and over 1 million men were killed, declared missing or injured during the summer and autumn in the Somme region. The Battle of Verdun lasted from February to December and was the longest battle of the war. At sea, the Battle of Jutland took place on the 31st May and 1st June which both sides claimed as a victory.

By the end of 1915 it was apparent that a voluntary system of enlistment was not going to maintain the troops required to win the war. The government passed the Military Service Act of 27nd January 1916 which brought in conscription for the first time.   Every British male subject who had attained the age of 19 years, and was not yet 41, and on the 2nd November 1915 was unmarried or a widower without dependent children, was deemed eligible to be enlisted into military service.

As a result, men were allocated to Classes which were connected to their year of birth. Class 1 was for those born in 1897 i.e. when they were 18 years of age. They were told they would not be called up until they were aged 19 (i.e. in 1916). Subsequently, Class 2 was for those born in 1896 and, depending on their birthday, they would have been called up in late 1915. The classes continued up to Class 23 for those born in 1875. Notices would be placed in prominent public spots and each man would be notified personally. It was the responsibility of the individual to present himself for duty at a given place, at a given time, on a given day.

The men from Howden-le-Wear who lost their lives during this year were:

Edward Browell, Elijah Lauder, John Slee, George Hagadorn, George Wearmouth, Arthur Gibson, George Sell, Alfred Wood, William Whitton, Henry Trimble and **Jack Kavanagh,**

Edward Browell

Edward Browell was born in 1886 at Mount Pleasant, Crook, son of Edward and Jane Browell. His father was born in Shincliffe, Durham, and his mother came from Ridedale in Cumberland. The Browell family was no stranger to tragedy since, of eight live births, only four of the children survived to adulthood. Edward's older brother David, who was a coal hewer and his wife Sarah Jane had married in 1903 and had one daughter, Edna, who had been born prematurely in 1907 and died later in the year.

Edward worked in the mines below ground from a very young age. He was a driver in 1901 at the age of 15 years. In 1910 Edward married Ruth Makepeace Myers and the 1911 Census shows he was living with his wife and his parents in Stanley, Crook. In May 1911 his son William was born, followed by another son, Henry, in 1915.

1911 Census showing Edward Browell living in four rooms with his wife and parents at 59 Ten Houses, Lower Stanley, Crook.
Image courtesy of www.ancestry.co.uk

Edward volunteered and enlisted in the army on the 13th May 1915 at the age of 29 years and 2 months, just 8 weeks before Henry was born. He was a typical Durham miner, being 5 ft 4½ ins tall and weighing 121 lbs, and was also of good physical development. On enlistment, his home address was recorded as 10 Valley Terrace, Howden-le-Wear. His army number was 10830 and he served with the 1st East Yorkshire Regiment. Edward travelled to France in August 1915. Ruth was receiving 21 shillings a week for her family, made up of 17s 6d separation allowance and 3s 6d that Edward allotted from his pay directly to Ruth.

The date of Edward's death was a few weeks before the Battle of the Somme which started on 1st July 1916, and there was much activity in the Somme area. The war diary does not show exactly where the East Yorkshire Regiment was fighting, but it does tell a little of the story of what happened to Edward. The weather was fine and sunny for the first week in June, but trench life was difficult. Each day there was very heavy bombardment being made on both front line trenches. The British trench experienced heavy shelling on the 1st, 2nd, 3rd and 4th June. There were no casualties on the first two days, but on the 3rd June a German raiding party entered allied trenches and captured the listening post. The war diary notes that there were no allied prisoners taken back to German trenches but, when they retreated, 17 soldiers of the East Yorkshires had been killed and 42 soldiers wounded.

Heavy shelling continued in the same area as the previous day during the 4th June and at 8.50pm about 100 German soldiers were seen advancing toward the allied trenches. An artillery barrage halted them in their tracks and they retreated. An allied raiding party was planned on the right of the line, but it also was repelled by German artillery fire. 2 officers and 2 other ranks were killed and 24 were wounded.

The records from Norfolk Cemetery, Becordel-Becourt, 2 miles from Albert, show that from the 1st East Yorkshire Regiment, the 2 officers killed were Lieutenant T. Townsend and 2nd Lieutenant S. Anson, and 19 soldiers, including Private Edward Browell, were buried along with a sapper from the Royal Engineers who was working with them in the trenches. They are all listed with their date of death being the 4th June, although the war diary says it was on the 3rd and 4th of the month. One of these men was Edward Browell and he was buried alongside his colleagues with whom he died after 1 year and 23 days' service.

Ruth later remarried and was Mrs Ruth Jackson living back at Mount Pleasant, Stanley, when she received Edward's scroll, death plaque and 1915 Star, Victory and British medals.

Elijah Lauder

Elijah and his brother Roderick were two of Joseph and Margaret Lauder's sons, born eight years apart and both destined to be lost during the Great War. They followed an older brother into the Army, Thomas William, who had enlisted in the Territorial Army when it was first established in 1908.

Their father was a miner, at one stage a deputy manager, whilst Margaret brought up an ever growing family. By 1911, sixteen children had been born, with twelve surviving. The males, when old enough to work, were employed as stone and coal miners, putters or workers at the brickyard. The family had lived in a variety of homes at Beechburn, Low Flat and Middle Row, and at Thistleflat in Crook.

Elijah was born in 1892, the fifth child, and grew up in a noisy household. In 1913, Elijah married Sarah Jane Hewitt and his only child, John Joseph Lauder, was born in July 1914.

Private Elijah Lauder enlisted in the Durham Light Infantry early in the war, probably around December 1914. His number was 3211. Elijah was sent overseas in January 1916 and, in the week or so prior to his death, the battalion's war diary describes raiding parties and patrols going out from the trenches. There was also a signalling dugout blown in with the occupants having a narrow escape and there were a number of men wounded by German snipers and from mortar attacks.

The diary records that at La Clytte on the 10th July telegrams of congratulations were received from the 2nd Army 5th Corps Headquarters and the 50th Divisional Headquarters upon the capture of a prisoner who was of great value and who was affording information as to enemy troops on their front.

Sadly the entry for July 14th 1916 was not so encouraging:

> *"Private Corns, Private Lauder and Private Stokeld of Y Company were killed in 0H trenches and Sergeant Watson of Y Company was seriously wounded."*

They died as part of raid by two officers, four non-commissioned officers, ten bombers and ten riflemen on a German trench. There was a small amount of bombing and rifle fire and the number of the enemy killed was four or five. A day later, on July 15th, the battalion was relieved by the 6th Northumberland Fusiliers and marched back behind the lines to a camp near Brolooze.

Private Corns from Bishop Auckland, Private Stokeld from Hartlepool and Private Elijah Lauder from Howden-le-Wear were buried in adjacent graves in Ridge Wood Military Cemetery. Elijah's name is inscribed on the Howden-le-Wear War Memorial.

John Henry Slee

John Henry Slee was born in 1881, the son of Joseph and Mary Ann Slee. He was part of a large family and had 11 siblings. The family lived in Valley Terrace, Howden-le-Wear. By 1901 he had moved to School Street and John was working as an underground miner. In 1904 he married Mary Jane Hutton and they moved to High Street. In 1909 their son Joseph Michael was born and by 1911 John was a hewer in the mine, one of the best paid jobs.

In military terms, little is known of the minutiae of Corporal Slee's activities as his Service Record has not survived, but his Medal Roll Card gives his Regiment as the 10th Battalion of the Yorkshire Regiment. His service number was 19459. John volunteered to join the army and by October 1915 he was fighting in France. He was soon promoted to corporal.

Corporal John Slee was 34 years of age when he died along with thousands of other allied servicemen on the 1st July 1916, the first day of the Battle of the Somme. His body was never found and he is remembered on the Thiepval Memorial which was erected to remember the Missing from the Somme battlefields. A brass tablet was placed in the Parish Church in Howden-le-Wear with the following inscription.

Sacred to the memory of
Corporal John Henry Slee
who at the call of King and Country
left all that was dear to him, endured hardness
faced danger, and finally passed out of the
sight of his men by the path of duty and
self-sacrifice giving up his life
at Fricourt July 1st 1916.

That others might live in freedom

This tablet is erected by his loving wife

From his birth in 1881, he had been one of Howden-le-Wear's own, living in Valley Terrace, School Street and High Street. The Slee family was large and his death must have affected many. He was survived by his parents and most of his siblings, and by Mary to whom he had been married for 11 years and his 7 year old son Joseph Michael.

> SLEE, Cpl. John Henry, 19459. 10th Bn. Yorkshire Regt. 1st July, 1916. Age 34. Son of Joseph and Mary Slee; husband of Mary Jane Slee, of 59, High St., Howden-le-Wear, Co. Durham.

Death notice of John Henry Slee.
Image Courtesy of the Auckland Chronicle July 1916

John's name is inscribed on the Howden-le-Wear War Memorial.

George Hagedorn

George Hagedorn was born in Sunderland in 1883, the son of Mary Jane and Adolph Peter Hagedorn. Adolph died in 1885 whilst serving in the Merchant Marine service. He was in his thirties and his wife was left to raise four children. The family lived in Whitehouse Crescent, Sunderland, and Mary Jane supported her children by working as a dressmaker.

By the age of 18, George was working as a general carter and employed by the Black family who lived in Canon Cockin Street in Sunderland. Robert Black, the head of the family, was himself a carter and employer of two.

In 1911, George was living at High Street, Howden-le-Wear, working as a brickyard labourer and had been married for four years to Margaret. He had lost his first son George, aged one, in 1910, but became a father again when his second son James was born in January 1913.

May 5th 1915 saw Private George Hagedorn leaving for France with the 10th King's Own Yorkshire Light Infantry, which led to his being at the Battle of the Somme. Zero hour on July 1st 1916 was at 07.30am when combined assaults were to be made on Mametz, La Boisselle and Fricourt. In the forefront of the attacking brigade were the 9th and 10th Battalions of the King's Own Yorkshire Light Infantry, with support from battalions of the Durham Light Infantry and the East Yorkshire Regiment.

In preparation for the assault, the immediate area ahead had been bombarded with shells in order to clear the way for the advance, and the 9th and 10th King's Own Yorkshire Light Infantry, including Private 22758 Hagedorn, secured a position outside Fricourt.

Incursions made by further brigades were not as successful and, on a day when so many lost their lives, it is not clear whether George Hagedorn ever reached Fricourt or was killed whilst holding position. His body was never found. He was yet another of Howden-le-Wear's men who is commemorated on the Thiepval Memorial.

HAGEDORN, Pte. George, 22758. 10th Bn. King's Own Yorkshire Light Inf. 1st July, 1916. Age 33. Husband of Margaret Jane Hagedorn, of 52, Low Beechburn, Crook, Co. Durham.

Index of Thiepval Memorial identifying George Hagedorn.

Margaret, living at 52 Low Beechburn, Crook, was informed that her husband was missing presumed dead and later received a widow's pension and George's memorial scroll, death plaque and his medals.

The family was to suffer more pain when George's younger brother Arthur Hagedorn was also killed during the conflict. He was serving with the 9th Battalion of the Cheshire Regiment when he was killed on the 6th June

1918. Arthur was buried in Chambrecy British Cemetery, near Reims in France. This cemetery was created after the Armistice when bodies were reinterred from other smaller graveyards in the area.

Private George Hagedorn's name was added to the Howden-le-Wear War Memorial.

George Wearmouth

On January 21st 1891, Richard Wearmouth and his wife Elizabeth (née Slater) of Quarry Burn, Hunwick, had a second son George, younger brother to 5 year old Joseph. Unfortunately four years later, in 1896, Elizabeth died, leaving the family without a wife and mother.

By 1901, the family had moved to North Bitchburn where they lived together with a domestic servant Hannah Close and her 1 year old son William. In 1904, Richard and Hannah married and William adopted the Wearmouth name. The family moved to 13 Helmington Terrace, Hunwick, by which time Joseph had left home and was working as a coal miner close by at Beechburn.

By 1911, 20 year old George had followed his father into the mines and was employed as a 'shifter'. The following year on October 5th he married Mary Anne Singlewood and they set up house at North Bitchburn. On 28th September 1913, they had a daughter Mary Elizabeth and on Christmas Day 1916 a son Wilfred Verdun was born six months after his father's death. Wilfred lived a long life and died in 2005 at Gloucester. Mary chose to include the name 'Verdun' for her son Wilfred, most probably after the battle where her beloved husband was killed.

George's army experience had started on the 7th September 1914, at the apparent age of 23 years 6 months. Private George Wearmouth enlisted in the 13th Battalion of the Durham Light Infantry as a private soldier with the number 18477.

George served in Britain for almost a year, but on the 25th August 1915, he crossed the English Channel to fight in France. When George was in France, Mary received a separation allowance of 21 shillings, plus 3s 6d allocation from George's pay. He had two weeks' home leave in March 1916.

On the 14th May 1916, George became attached to the 68th Machine Gun Corps as a qualified machine gunner and was fighting in the protracted battle of Verdun. Sadly he was not to survive the war and on 10th July 1916 he was reported missing at the age of aged 25 years. George is commemorated at the Thiepval Memorial and on the Howden-le-Wear War Memorial.

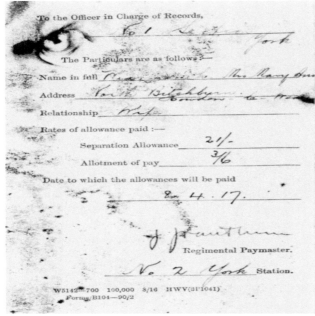

Army Form identiying the separation allowance paid by the Army to Mary Anne with the voluntary addition of 3s 6d from George allocated from his pay.

The second form was included with George's belongings, his disc and photos, that were returned to Mary Anne in May 1917.

Images courtesy of www.ancestry.co.uk

Mary Anne was awarded a widow's pension of 18s 9d for herself and her children and in 1918 she moved to 10 Victoria Street (Row), Howden-le-Wear, where she married a local farmer's son from Pit Close Farm, Thomas Charleton.

Mrs Charleton took receipt of her late husband's medals and personal effects and carried on bringing up her two children. She duly registered them at Howden-le-Wear school for their education. Wilfred Verdun Wearmouth was entered in the Admission Register on the 9th January 1922 and went up to the Mixed Department on 1st April 1924. Mary Elizabeth was registered by Thomas Charleton on 30th September 1918 into the Infant Department but left on the 17th February 1919 to attend Witton Park school. On the 9th January 1923, Mary returned to Howden Mixed School.

Arthur Gibson

In 1911, 17 year old Arthur Gibson lived with his 53 year old father Joseph, 41 year old mother Maggie, 15 year old brother Joseph and 4 year old brother George at 'Loves Beechburn' now known as Greenhead, between Howden-le-Wear and Fir Tree. His father was a carter working on a farm while Arthur and Joseph were working as pony drivers in the Beechburn coal mine.

On 13th February 1915, Arthur, aged 21 years, passed the Medical Examination 'fit to serve with good vision and physical development' and duly enlisted at Bishop Auckland into the 1st/6th Battalion of the Durham Light Infantry. His number was 3423.

He had signed up for the *'duration of war'* and, although initially in the reserve forces, he agreed to serve in any place outside of the UK in the event of National Emergency. Consequently on 10th July 1916 Arthur sailed with his battalion from Southampton to Le Havre where he proceeded to join the 15th Battalion DLI.

Private Arthur Gibson.
Image courtesy of the Auckland Chronicle

Only 7 days later, on 17th July 1916, he was killed in action in the field and his body was never recovered. Leaving his father Joseph, brothers Joseph, aged 22, and George, aged 13, living at 28 Long Row, Greenhead, Howden-le-Wear, it appears his mother may have died. Meanwhile, his grandmother Mary Donohue was living on Newton Cap Bank, Bishop Auckland.

Arthur is commemorated on the Menin Gate Memorial at Ypres and also on Howden-le-Wear War Memorial.

George Sell

George Sell was born at Ulrome, near Hornsea in the East Riding of Yorkshire, during 1896, to Alfred and Kate Sell. Alfred was an agricultural labourer and, by 1901, he and Kate had another two children, John born in 1898 and Pretoria born in 1901. Her name was probably given in remembrance of the town of Pretoria in South Africa during the Boer War.

By 1911, the family had increased as there were another four children: Harold born in 1903, Herbert born in 1905, Thomas born in 1908 and Edward born in 1910. George was no longer living at home but was working as a 15 year old servant to Anthony Burdon, a farmer at Bradbury near Ferryhill, in County Durham.

Private George Sell.
Image courtesy of NER WWI Roll of Honour, York

George went on to be employed as a platelayer on the North Eastern Railway Company on the Bishop Auckland - Crook line. There is no link to his being resident in Howden-le-Wear, but it could be that, as a railway worker, he was living in lodgings in the village.

George enlisted in the Durham Light Infantry with the number 33676 in September 1914. At some time he transferred to be a gunner with the Royal Field Artillery and served with the 53rd Howitzer Brigade, 'A' Battery.

Beechburn for Howden-le-Wear Station c 1900. Waiting room and toilets on the platform for trains arriving from Bishop Auckland and travelling to Crook, Tow Law and beyond.

Image courtesy of Howden-le- Wear History Society

A section of North Eastern Railway at Beechburn for Howden-le-Wear showing the platelayers' cabin in the foreground where George Sell most likely worked. *Image courtesy of Howden-le-Wear History Society*

George was killed on the Somme on the 24th July 1916 and was buried in Quarry Cemetery, Montauban. He is also remembered on the Howden-le-Wear War Memorial and on the North East Railway Roll of Honour in York where it states:

'Gunner George Sell, Royal Field Artillery, was killed in action abroad on July 24th. 1916. Mr Sell, who was 21 years old, joined the NER service as platelayer at Beechburn on May 18th 1914 and enlisted in September 1914.'

The North Eastern Railway Memorial in York with George Sell's name.
Image courtesy of Howden-le-Wear History Society

As much of the heavy artillery, ammunition and supplies were transported and manoeuvred at the front on temporary rail tracks, George Sell's knowledge of plate-laying would have been in demand and he may have been employed in this capacity.

Although George was thought to be associated with Howden-le-Wear for only a short time, he must have made an impact on the community to have his name engraved on the village War Memorial.

A poppy wreath placed on the North Eastern Railway Memorial in York.
Image courtesy of Howden-le-Wear History Society

Alfred Wood

From the outset the research concerning 'A Wood S.R.' named on the Howden-le-Wear War Memorial proved challenging for two specific reasons. Firstly, it was difficult to find a record of the Wood family in Howden-le-Wear, and secondly, there appeared to be no match for 'A Wood S.R.' in the military archives.

Nevertheless, further research revealed that the 1911 Census shows a Wood family 'headed' by Sarah Ann Wood. Her husband Frederick Wood had died since the previous Census of 1901. The family lived at High Street, Howden-le-Wear, there were five children in the family, and Alfred was the second oldest, aged 19. It is highly likely that this was the Wood family who lost their son Alfred during the conflict.

Although research into Alfred's family history made progress, the problem was that a direct military match could not be found for 'A Wood'.

The 'S.R' recorded on the War Memorial (denoting his regiment) could have identified him as being in the Special Reserve or in the Signals Regiment. However, further research highlighted the possibility that his regiment may have been the Scottish Rifles.

There is evidence of a George Alfred Wood serving in the 10th Battalion of the Cameronians, which was also known as the Scottish Rifles. This Alfred volunteered, was sent to France on 12th December 1915, and died on

42

the 12th August 1916 in the Somme Region. His body was not found but he is remembered on the Thiepval Memorial. Unfortunately, there is no trace of this Alfred Wood having any connection with Howden-le-Wear.

The Medal Roll Card of Private George Alfred Wood from the 10th Battalion of the Scottish Rifles, who was killed in Action in France.

Image courtesy of www.ancestry.co.uk

Therefore, although there is clear evidence of Alfred Wood and his family living in Howden-le-Wear, his military career remains a mystery.

Alfred's father was called Frederick Wood and his mother was Sarah Ann. The 1911 Census identifies Sarah Ann as being a 'widow' and having some six children. They were Joseph, aged 22, Alfred, aged 19, Frederick, aged 17, Amelia, aged 14, George, aged 12, and Elsie Maud, aged 12. All the children were recorded as being born in Thornaby. The family lived in a four roomed house in High Street, Howden-le-Wear. Alfred was identified as being an 'oil hawker' on his own account, his older brother Joseph worked as a 'coal mine hewer', and Frederick junior was 'a miner's putter'. The younger siblings appear to have been 'in education.'

Looking further back into the family history in 1861, Alfred's grandparents were living in 2 Town Head, Northallerton, North Yorkshire. At that time Alfred's father Frederick was only 1 year old. Alfred's grandfather Thomas was head of the family, aged 33, and he was employed as a 'shoemaker master' and his grandmother was called Ellen. Alfred's grandparents were both born in Northallerton, Thomas in 1828 and Ellen in 1830.

43

In 1871, Alfred's father Frederick still lived at the same address and his grandfather Thomas appeared to be employed as a 'fruiter'. However, in this Census there is no record of Alfred's grandmother Ellen who was probably away from home on the Census night. Nevertheless, there was an additional child in the family called Camellia, aged 7.

By 1881, Frederick was still single and living with his parents at 5 Main Street, Northallerton. He was aged 21, employed as a labourer, and had a younger brother called Albert. His father Thomas is again recorded as a' shoemaker' and his mother Ellen is again recorded with the family.

By the time of the 1891 Census, Frederick had married Sarah Ann Wason (or Wayson) and they were living in Thornaby at 10, Whalley Street. Frederick appears to have been employed as a 'plasterer's helper'. They had three children, Heather, aged 6, Edith, aged 4, and Joseph, aged 2. Also living with them was Frederick's older brother Alfred, aged 34, who was employed as a labourer. In addition there was a lodger called John Pearson, also aged 34, who appeared to be employed as 'furnace man'.

The 1901 Census records Alfred's father Frederick as being aged 40, and a 'general labourer'. The Wood family was now living at Witton Park. However it appears that Frederick senior died between 1901 and 1911 and Sarah Wood is now recorded as head of the household.

Research into the history of Alfred's mother Sarah Ann Wason (or Wayson) shows that she was born in 1860. The 1861 Census has her recorded as living at 9 Bank Top Houses in Eldon. The household consisted of two married couples and Sarah Ann. The head of the household was James Jacques, aged 23, and his wife was Elizabeth, aged 22. There was William Wason, a coal miner, aged 21, and Martha Wason, aged 18. William and Martha were recorded as being 'visitors' and were born in Scotland and Westmorland respectively. Sarah Ann was aged 1 and recorded as a being a 'niece'. Therefore she was the daughter of William and Martha and related to the Jacques family.

In 1871, the Wayson family were recorded as living in Riverside Houses, Monkwearmouth, near Sunderland, with Sarah Ann having two younger brothers, Joseph, aged 7, and John, aged 4. William was recorded as being employed as an 'iron stone cutter' and Martha was a 'dressmaker'.

By 1881 Sarah Ann, now aged 20, was employed as a domestic servant for the Dawson family who lived in Thorntree House, Middleton St George. William Dawson, aged 38, was the head of the household. He was a coal merchant, and he had been born in Hunwick, only 2 miles from Howden-le-

Wear. Priscilla Dawson had been born in Sadberge, which is near to Middleton St George.

At the time of the 1891 Census, Sarah Ann is recorded as the 'wife' of Frederick Wood as they had been married in 1883.

Summarising these details, we see that Alfred Wood's father Frederick was born in Northallerton in 1860 and his mother Sarah Ann was also born in 1860, but in Coundon. Frederick lived in Northallerton until 1881, and at that time Sarah Ann was a domestic servant living in Middleton St George. They married in 1883 and by 1891 the family had moved to Thornaby.

In 1901 they were living in Escomb, and by 1911 they were at Howden-le-Wear. Given that Frederick was employed as 'a general labourer', it appears that the family moved to places associated with the iron and steel industry. At this time the average worker would usually have to live within walking distance of his employment. Therefore when Frederick moved to a new address, this could have been to be near to the heavy industrial sites in Teesside, Witton Park and Crook. Alfred's father died before the 1911 Census and it is not known when the family moved to Howden-le Wear.

By the time of the 1911 Census, Sarah Ann was recorded as head of the Wood family. Her eldest son Joseph was employed as a 'coal miner hewer', Alfred as an 'oil hawker' and Frederick Jnr was a 'miner putter'. The three youngest children, Amelia, George and Elsie Maud, were in education. Together Sarah and Frederick Wood had had eight children and in the 1911 Census it is recorded they had all survived. Given the infant mortality rate for working class people during the late 19th century, this was a remarkable achievement.

At the outbreak of WWI Alfred would have been eligible for conscription at the age of 22.

It is at this point that the research comes to an end. There is no doubt Alfred Wood was living in Howden-le-Wear just prior to the outbreak of war, and that he would have been eligible for army service in 1914. However, along with many other WWI soldiers, his military records and the actual circumstances which led up to his death are untraceable. 60% of all the WWI records were lost during the London blitz in 1940.

William Whitton

William Whitton, known as Willie, was born in Witton-le-Wear in the early months of 1895 and was the only son of William and Suzannah Whitton. He had an older sister called Edie (Edith) who was born in 1892. Sadly Suzannah died within a year of Willie's birth. William remarried a lady from Stanhope called Priscilla Carrick and they had two daughters, Doris and Mary, who were Edie's and Willie's half-sisters.

The family lived at Victoria Cottages, Howden-le-Wear, until William Whitton moved the family to the pipe works at North Bitchburn, when he became the manager of North Bitchburn Fireclay Company.

Willie went to school in High Grange until the age of 14 and then left school to take up a position as a labourer/sanitary pipe worker, as shown in the 1911 Census. The family was staunch Methodist, being very involved with the Wesleyan Chapel at Wear Valley Junction. Indeed, the family later donated a table to this chapel, bearing a brass plaque to honour Willie's memory. This may now be seen at Howden-le-Wear Methodist Chapel, having been brought there via the Wesleyan Chapel in Howden-le-Wear which is now The New Victoria Centre.

Willie Whitton as a young man about town.
Image courtesy of Anthea Agar

Willie's service record has not survived, but from his Medal Roll Card it is apparent that he enlisted in Bishop Auckland before conscription, his regimental number being 6/3829, and he joined the 6th Durham Light Infantry.

The Medal Roll Card of Private William Whitton.

Image courtesy of www.ancestry.co.uk

Willie did not have perfect eyesight, and the family hoped that he would not be accepted for the services; however, this was not to be the case. As he left Howden-le-Wear railway station, after embarkation leave to travel overseas, Priscilla, Willie's step-mother, was reported as saying that she felt that this would be the last time she would see Willie. Sadly she was proved correct.

Willie took part in the Battle of Fler-Courcelette, an offensive on the Somme with the 1st/6th Durham Light Infantry. This battle started on 15th September 1916 and lasted about one week until 20th September. The strategic objective of a break through the German lines was not achieved, although this offensive was considered a success as an advance of 2,500 to 3,500 yards was achieved, but at what cost?

This was to be the third and final general offensive in this area mounted by the British. However, fighting would continue on the Somme for a further two months. William was killed on the second day of this offensive, 16th September 1916, in the 21st year of his life along with another 24 soldiers and a number of officers.

Private Willie Whitton proudly wearing his DLI uniform.

Image courtesy of Anthea Agar

Thousands of British servicemen lost their lives in the Somme area of France, and were buried in war graves in the area, but Private Willie Whitton 3829 of the Durham Light Infantry, along with over 70,000 other soldiers who fought on the Somme, has no known grave, and therefore he is remembered on the Memorial at Thiepval.

The Thiepval Memorial - William Whitton's name is recorded on Pier and Face 14A and 15C with other D.L.I. names.

Private Whitton's name on the Thiepval Memorial, which remembers the fallen from the Somme with no known grave. Willie's family wrote on the photograph after visiting France.
Image courtesy of Dorothy Longstaff

He is also remembered, along with 30 other WWI servicemen, on the War Memorial in his home village of Howden-le-Wear. Willie is specially thought of each Remembrance Sunday at Howden-le-Wear Methodist Chapel, when a poppy is placed on "his" table.

Henry Trimble

Amelia Clark of 18 Victoria Row, Howden-le-Wear, lost both husband George and eldest son Robert Taylor in the conflict and she was to share her grief with her next door neighbours, John and Mary Ann Trimble. Mr and Mrs Trimble also had the misfortune of losing their eldest son Henry in the same conflict.

Census records refer to the family as 'Tremble' but the army records adopt the name 'Trimble'. By careful cross-referencing of the names of other family members, it has been possible to identify and confirm the correct relationships.

In 1894, John Tremble from Tow Law married Mary Ann from Woodside, Witton Park, and by 1914 Mary Ann had borne eleven children, three of whom had died at birth or in infancy. The eight surviving offspring were Mary Alice, Henry, Owen, William, Michael, Gladys, Badelia and Vincent.

In 1911, nine of them were living in a three roomed house at 221 Langley Moor, having moved there from Crook via Coxhoe. John Tremble worked as a coal hewer and his eldest son Henry, aged only 15 years, also worked in the mines as a driver, and he would have the job of driving a pit pony hauling loaded tubs of coal through the tunnels of the mine.

The family moved again and by 1914 were all living next door to the Clark family at number 17 Victoria Row, Howden-le-Wear. Father and son probably worked together at the North Beechburn Colliery complex adjacent to the row of houses.

Fortunately, some of the military records that have survived show details of Henry Trimble's army service and from faded documents it has been possible to extract some details of his War Service.

Following the declaration of war in 1914, on 7th September, young Henry Tremble, aged 18 years, enlisted at Bishop Auckland. He declared his age as 19 years old, passed the medical examination and was declared fit for service in the Durham Light Infantry.

5 ft 3 ins tall Private Trimble, Number 14570, joined the newly formed 15th (Service) Battalion at Newcastle as part of the Third New Army and then moved to Halton Park and joined the 6th Brigade of the 21st Division on the 7th January 1915. He was inoculated and received his vaccinations on the 2nd March in readiness for posting to France. In April 1915, the battalion moved to Witley in Surrey.

Army Form W. 5080.

Regiment .... DURHAM LIGHT INFTY.

To be filled in by
Officer in Charge of
Records.

.... deceased

STATEMENT of the Names and Addresses of all the Relatives of the above-named deceased
Soldier in each of the degrees specified below that are now living.

NOTE.—Against those degrees of relationship in which there is no relative now living the word "none" is to be inserted. If the
answers are not filled in, much correspondence and delay may be occasioned by the neglect.

Degree of relationship		NAMES IN FULL of every relative now living in each degree enquired for (see note above).	ADDRESS IN FULL of each surviving relative opposite his or her name.
Widow of the Soldier		None	
Children of the Soldier and dates of their births... ...		None	
Father of the Soldier		John Trimble	17 Victoria Row, Howden-Le-Wear
Mother of the Soldier		Mary Ann Trimble	Victoria Row, Howden-Le-Wear
Brothers of the Soldier	Full Blood	Vincent Trimble 4	do - do -
		Owen Trimble 22	Victoria Row, Howden-le-Wear
	Half blood	William Trimble 17	Victoria Row, Howden-le-Wear
		Michael Trimble 13	Victoria Row, Howden-le-Wear
Sisters of the Soldier	Full blood	Mary Alice 25	Victoria Row, Howden-le-Wear
		Gladys May 10	Victoria Row, Howden-le-Wear
	Half blood ...		

If **no** Relatives in the degrees above are **now** living the following particulars should be given :—

	Names of those now living.		Addresses in full.
Grandparents of the Soldier ...			
Nephews and Nieces of the Soldier		Age	
Uncles and Aunts by blood of the Soldier (not Uncles and Aunts by marriage)			

DECLARATION.

I hereby declare that the above is a true and complete Statement of all the Relatives of the late Soldier now
living in the degrees enquired for.

John Trimble Signature of the Declarant.

Relationship to the Soldier .... Father

Address in full .... 17 Victoria Row, Howden-le-Wear

I hereby certify that the above Statement and Declaration made by *John Trimble*
and signed in my presence is complete and correct, to the best of my knowledge and belief.

Dated at Howden-le-Wear this 25th day of August 1919.

Signature of Minister or Magistrate. *Bertram Ive Spencer* Qualification Clerk in Holy orders

Address The Vicarage, Howden-le-Wear

6527. Wt. W5795/PB1. 1,000,000. 2/19. S.O./P.B4.

**Private Henry Trimble's army records show his family being his father,
mother, two brothers (full blood), two brothers and two sisters (half blood),
all living in Howden-le-Wear.** *Image courtesy of www.ancestry.co.uk*

After a short 3 days' home leave from 7th to 10th September, on 11th
September 1915, the battalion was mobilised for war and landed at
Boulogne. They were soon engaged in various actions on the Western

Front, including in 1915 The Battle of Loos where the division suffered over 3,000 casualties and took the rest of the year to rebuild.

It was during one of these encounters that Private Trimble was injured by a gun-shot wound to his left ankle. He recovered and, following further home leave, he rejoined his battalion on the 6th April 1916.

On 1st July, supported by a French attack to the south, thirteen divisions of Commonwealth forces launched an offensive on a line from north of Gommecourt to Maricourt. Despite a preliminary bombardment lasting seven days, the German defences were barely touched and the attack met unexpectedly fierce resistance. Losses were catastrophic and, with only minimal advances on the southern flank, the initial attack was a failure.

In the following weeks huge resources of manpower and equipment were deployed in an attempt to exploit the modest successes of the first day. However, the German Army resisted tenaciously, and repeated attacks and counter attacks meant a major battle for every village, copse and farmhouse gained. At the end of September, Thiepval was finally captured but, during one of these confrontations, Private Henry Trimble was killed in action on 16th September 1916. His body was never recovered and identified.

Private Henry Trimble's army records show that he enlisted on the 7th September 1914, and show his various posting dates.
Image courtesy of www.ancestry.co.uk

On 7th February 1917 an order was issued that any articles of personal property belonging to Private Henry Trimble should be despatched to Mrs Mary Anne Trimble at 17 Victoria Row. The order was stamped by Infantry Records in York, *'NO EFFECTS'* which implied that no belongings had been recovered to return to his mother.

Copy of the record stating that there were 'NO EFFECTS' to be returned to Henry Trimble's mother. How sad that must have made the family.
Image courtesy of www.ancestry.co.uk

She would in due course receive his British War Medal and Victory Medal and the memorial scroll and plaque. According to Army Paymaster records at York, Mrs Trimble was also in receipt of an allotment of Henry's pay, 3s 6d until 2nd October 1916.

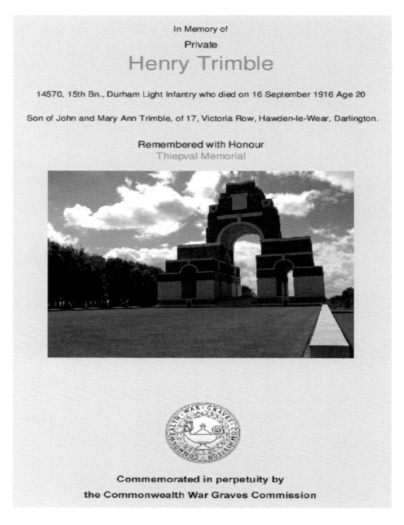

In Memory of
Private
Henry Trimble

14570, 15th Bn., Durham Light Infantry who died on 16 September 1916 Age 20

Son of John and Mary Ann Trimble, of 17, Victoria Row, Hawden-le-Wear, Darlington.

Remembered with Honour
Thiepval Memorial

Commemorated in perpetuity by
the Commonwealth War Graves Commission

The certificate issued by the CWGC on its website for Private Henry Trimble remembering his name on the Thiepval Memorial.

Image courtesy of www.cwgc.org

Private Henry Trimble is commemorated on the Thiepval Memorial and also on Howden-le-Wear War Memorial in the village.

The Trimble family continued to live at Victoria, in Howden-le-Wear, and John registered Henry's sister Gladys on 20th August 1913 in the Infant Department at Howden-le-Wear school before she moved to High Grange school on the 16th July 1915. Vincent, Henry's youngest brother, was also admitted to Howden-le-Wear school on the 19th January 1920 before moving up to the Mixed School on the 31st March 1922.

Jack Kavanagh

John William ("Jack") Kavanagh was born in Howden-le-Wear on the 5th January 1890. The record of his birth shows his name spelt with an initial 'C', and this discrepancy occurs elsewhere.

The Census of 1891, again recording the surname with an initial 'C', shows the family living in Church Street in Howden-le-Wear. His father Michael, a coal miner, aged 28, originally came from Cumberland, and his mother Margaret, aged 25, came from the neighbouring village of Witton-le-Wear. Jack had an older sister, Jane, aged 4.

The Census of 1901 records the surname with an initial 'K', and shows the family living in Valley Terrace, Howden-le-Wear. Michael Kavanagh was still a coal miner, and the family had increased with the birth of Jack's two brothers, George, aged 8, and Benjamin, aged 10 months, and sister Mary, aged 3, who died when she was only 6 years old.

At the time of the 1911 Census the family was still living in Valley Terrace, Howden-le-Wear. Michael was still a coal miner, but had been promoted to deputy overman at Bitchburn (also known as Beechburn) Colliery, which was literally on his doorstep in Howden-le-Wear. Jack, now aged 21, was a boiler minder at the same colliery. In this Census, the transcribed version shows him as John M, but the copy of the original Census quite clearly shows John Wm.

There are no details of Jack Kavanagh's date of enlistment, or of his initial training as a stoker. However, a nephew of his has said that he served in the Battle of Jutland from 31st May - 1st June 1916.

This photograph shows Stoker Kavanagh with the name H.M.S. VICTORY on his cap band. This was the name of the barracks at Portsmouth which acted as a holding base for men who were posted into the Portsmouth area, and was also a training base.

Image courtesy of Douglas Kavanagh

There are more details dating from the time when he trained as a stoker at the Royal Naval Base at Portsmouth. It is known at this time he was a Stoker 1st Class, which implies that he had already been in the Navy for some time. His official hardback training note book, which his nephew still possesses, has Jack's own writing on the inside of the front cover stating:

Stoker I John Kavanagh,
Hostilities
R. N B [sic]
Portsmouth

This book, reminiscent of a student's exercise book, shows his training as a stoker for oil fired turbines, with a series of questions and answers, all in his own neat handwriting, and some precise and detailed drawings.

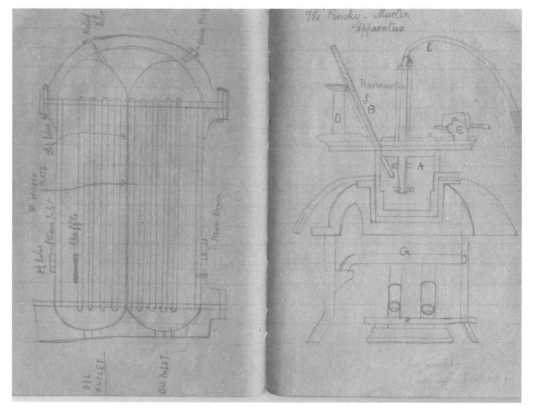

Pages from Stoker Kavanagh's training note book.

Image courtesy of Douglas Kavanagh

It is interesting to note, however, that, while we tend to think of stokers as men shovelling coal, his training was as a stoker for the new oil fired turbine engines. Is it fair to assume that he had already spent some time on coal fired ships, and was now undergoing training for the new oil fired vessels?

In October, 1916, Jack was serving as a Stoker, 1st class, on *H.M.S. Amazon*. This was a Tribal-class destroyer launched in 1908. One of the policies of the First Sea Lord in 1904 was that there should be a new type of destroyer capable of steaming at over 30 knots, and burning oil fuel rather than coal. She was stationed at Dover during the First World War, serving in both the North Sea and the English Channel.

From August to October 1916, she was part of the 6th Destroyer Flotilla, Dover Patrol. She spent much of September at Portsmouth being scraped, painted and refitted. Having taken on fuel oil and ammunition, she passed out of Portsmouth on the 24th September to carry out sea trials, including the practice firing of torpedoes. The ship's log for the 25th September records that on that day seven stokers joined the ship from Haslar Camp, although we are not given their names. We do not know whether or not Jack Kavanagh was one of these, or whether he was already serving on *H.M.S. Amazon*. *H.M.S. Amazon* left Portsmouth for Dover on the 26th September. In the course of the following four weeks she made various patrols from Dover, including several to Dunkirk and one to Boulogne.

Having spent four weeks carrying out routine patrols, *H.M.S. Amazon* was now to be involved in action in what came to be known as the Battle of Dover Strait on the 26th - 27th October 1916, when two and a half flotillas of German torpedo boats from the Flanders Flotilla launched a raid into the Dover Strait in an attempt to disrupt the Dover Barrage and destroy whatever Allied shipping could be found in the Strait.

For some time, one of the risks of which the Admiralty was continually conscious was the possibility that the German forces might try to force the

Stoker Jack Kavanagh with another seaman whilst serving on HMS Victory.
Image courtesy of Douglas Kavanagh

defences of the Dover Strait. Despite the fact that the German High Seas Fleet had suffered losses in the Battle of Jutland and needed to be reconstructed, and it would therefore be difficult for it to provide the necessary cover for a major attack, there was pressure on the German commanders to take some offensive action as the British anti-submarine forces were taking a toll on their U-boats, and a limited offensive against the British might help to interfere with these successes. A raiding attack was therefore planned, and the 3rd and 9th Torpedo Boat Flotilla left Germany for Zeebrugge during the night of the 23rd October. The Admiralty realised that some German naval movement was happening, but assumed that it would take place in Flanders Bight.

Owing to a previous lack of large German torpedo boats, the Flanders Flotilla had not attempted to make any raids against the Dover Patrol in several months, and, as a result, British defences were quite lax in the area, but the presence of more than 20 large German torpedo boats meant that the balance of power was now in the Germans' favour.

On the night of the 26th October the Germans launched a raid into the Dover Strait. Approaching the barrage, the German torpedo boats were challenged and engaged by the British destroyer *H.M.S. Flirt*, which was destroyed. The Germans successfully attacked the drifters, but were then challenged and engaged by a flotilla of six British Tribal-class destroyers, including *H.M.S. Amazon*, sent to repel them. As a result of a "misinterpretation" of orders, the British ships failed to stay together as a concentrated force and became increasingly scattered, thus weakening their effectiveness. In the battle, the British suffered heavy losses, with two vessels sunk and several, including three destroyers, damaged.

HMS *Amazon* on which Stoker Jack Kavanagh served.
Image courtesy of www.naval-history.net

One of the destroyers damaged was *H.M.S. Amazon*. At the time of the attack at 12.50am on the morning of the 27th October, Jack Kavanagh was off duty, but crew members off duty were tasked with carrying shells up to the deck to the guns during an attack. As Jack was carrying a shell over the deck, a German shell hit *H.M.S. Amazon* and he was thrown backwards to a stair well, receiving fatal injuries to the back of his head.

The Germans were successful in fighting off the British ships, before making a successful withdrawal. Only one of their ships was damaged, and there were no casualties.

H.M.S. Amazon returned to Dover, securing to No 50 buoy at 2.30am. Eight members of her crew who had been injured were discharged to hospital at 3.10am and later in the morning at 11.15am the bodies of the five crew members who had been killed, including that of Stoker Kavanagh, were discharged.

H.M.S. Amazon left Dover the following afternoon for Sheerness, and continued to Chatham the next morning. A barracks working party started work on her on the morning of the 30th October. She continued to serve in the Navy, but was sold after the war on the 22nd October, 1919.

Jack Kavanagh's body was returned by train to Howden-le-Wear. Joseph Gibson, the undertaker, took a Union flag from the church and draped it over the coffin before removing it from the station.

There was an instruction with the coffin that it should not be opened, no doubt to prevent people seeing the injuries to Jack's head. His mother said that she wanted the coffin opened so that she could be sure that it was indeed her son who was inside. Mr Gibson assured her that he would confirm this.

John William Kavanagh was buried in a Commonwealth War Grave in the churchyard of St Mary the Virgin, Howden-le-Wear, on the 2nd November 1916, aged 26. The details in Fir Tree parish records, no.1593, show that he was accepted home by J. Gibson. The service was conducted by the Reverend William Herbert Parkes, Vicar of St Mary's Church. It is interesting to note that he had a Church of England funeral service, even though his family was, at least nominally, Roman Catholic.

Jack was engaged to be married. His mother still lived in Valley Terrace in Howden-le-Wear at the time of his death, and she used to visit his grave every Sunday morning and put on it flowers which she had purchased from Bradley's florists opposite the Co-operative store in Bishop Auckland.

John William Kavanagh, the only Royal Navy casualty listed on the War Memorial, was awarded the Victory Medal and the British War Medal.

In Memory of
Stoker 1st Class JOHN WILLIAM KAVANAGH

K/29118, H.M.S. "Amazon.", Royal Navy
who died age 26
on 27 October 1916
Son of Michael and Margaret Kavanagh, of Howden-le-Wear, Co.
Durham.
Remembered with honour
HOWDEN-LE-WEAR (ST. MARY) CHURCHYARD

Commemorated in perpetuity by
the Commonwealth War Graves Commission

Image courtesy of the www.cwgc.org.

Jack Kavanagh's Victory and British War Medals.
Image courtesy of Douglas Kavanagh

❖ *1917*

1917 in Germany the policy was reintroduced of unrestricted submarine warfare which caused much fear in the allied shipping lanes, but ultimately was the catalyst that brought America into the war in April. Many allied ships and also merchant ships were attacked and lost.

Battles on land included Arras, Vimy Ridge and a major allied offensive at the Messines Ridge followed by Paschendaele.

The Eastern Front became more haphazard after the internal revolution within Russia, and Tsar Nicholas abdicated in March. Lenin became the leader in November, and a peace pact was agreed with the Central Powers in December.

The British were still fighting in Iraq and in March Baghdad was captured and in July the Arabs, along with T.E. Lawrence, later known as Lawrence of Arabia, captured Aquaba.

The first American troops arrived in France in June increasing the allied manpower on the ground.

The Battle of Cambrai on the Western Front in November was the first successful tank battle for the British.

The men from Howden-le-Wear who lost their lives during this year were:

Alfred Bridges, Frank Reid, John Hook, Henry Walker, **Sydney Luck, Thomas Horn, Thomas Evans, David Etherington, Jonathon Bell,** Gordon Parkin** and **Thomas Robinson.**

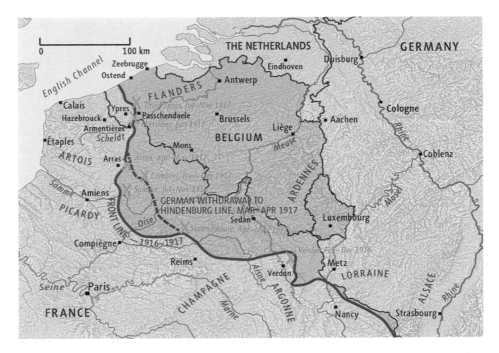

Map highlighting the fighting areas in Northern France and Belgium during 1917. *Image courtesy of www.1914-1918.net*

Alfred Bridges

Alfred was born in 1896 to Alfred and Maria Susannah Bridges and they lived at 58 Low Beechburn, Crook. They had 4 children, Alfred, Annie born in 1898, Francis born 1902 and Samuel born in 1905. By 1911, Alfred was working alongside his father in the colliery as a 'helper up in the mine'. Alfred senior was the colliery timekeeper.

Alfred enlisted as a driver in the Royal Field Artillery with the number 3263 and 751174 when they renumbered the servicemen during the conflict.

By the time he died on the 18th January 1917, he was a gunner with the 250th Brigade Royal Field Artillery.

Alfred was one of five soldiers who died on the 18th January 1917, buried at St Sever Cemetery Extension in Rouen. There was a large general hospital at Rouen and it is highly possible that Alfred had been wounded and later died as a result of his wounds. He was only 20 when he died.

His gravestone had the words 'Peace, Perfect Peace' engraved on the bottom, paid for by his mother in his memory. Families were allowed to add text to the gravestones if they wished at the cost of 3½ pence per letter.

Private Alfred Bridges' name was placed on the Howden-le-Wear War Memorial by his parents and siblings, and he was awarded the Victory and British War Medal.

Medal Roll Card for Driver Alfred Bridges.

Image courtesy of www.ancestry.co.uk

Frank Reid

In 1858, James Reid was born in Ballylinnie, Antrim, Ireland. At some time in the 1880s he left the family home in the search for employment. His travels brought him to Crook, County Durham, where the coal mines and associated coke works were in full production. James found work as a 'coke oven cooler', probably at the Bank Foot Works.

Early in 1888 he married Mary Anne Grey and they set up home in Grey Street, Crook, where they brought up seven children in a three roomed house.

By1911 there were James and Mary Ann with son John, aged 22, and daughter Agnes, aged 20, who had both left home, Margaret (Maggie), aged

18 years, Frank, aged 15 years, Andrew, aged 9 years, Maude Annie, aged 5 years, and James, aged 3 years.

By the time war broke out in 1914, Frank Reid had married and he and his wife lived at 22 Stable Row, Loves Beechburn (Greenhead), between Crook and Howden-le-Wear. He would probably be working at the local coal mine or brickyard.

Private Frank Reid enlisted in the Durham Light Infantry 1st/6th Battalion as Private Number 3476 and later with Number 250401. Little is known of his army career, but on 24th February 1917 he was killed in action in France at Flanders.

The DLI 1st/6th Battalion was a Territorial Force formed on the 4th August 1914 stationed at Bishop Auckland before moving to Bolden Colliery. On 17th April 1915 they were mobilised for war and landed at Boulogne.

On 14th May 1915 the Battalion became part of the151st Brigade of the 50th Division and engaged in various actions on the Western Front, including The Battle of St. Julien, The Battle of Frezenburg Ridge and The Battle of Bellewaarde Ridge.

On 3rd June 1915, as a result of severe casualties at Ypres, they amalgamated with the 1st/8th Battalion to form the 6th/8th Battalion.

On the 11th August they resumed their individual regimental identities once replacement soldiers arrived and were involved in the Battle of Fler-Courcelette, the Battle of Morval and the Battle of the Transloy Ridges.

Private Frank Reid was eventually buried with honour at the Assevillers New British Cemetery. This cemetery was created after the Armistice and bodies were brought from other smaller burial sites and reinterred. It is highly probable that Frank was initially buried in Kiboko Wood Cemetery, Biaches, where 30 British soldiers were buried in February and March 1917, of whom 20 belonged to the 1st/6th Battalion of the Durham Light Infantry.

Frank Reid is also commemorated on the Howden-le-Wear War Memorial.

13
WILL.

In the event of my Death I give the whole of my property and effects to my wife

Signed   Mrs F. Reid
Pte. F. Reid 22 Stable Row
No 3046 Loves Beechburn
6th D.L.I. Nr Crook
Colvsham
England

John Hook

In the 1901 census John Hook, aged 4, was the only child of Walter and Annie Hook. He was born in1897 at Stable Row, which was also known as Park Terrace, Howden-le-Wear, in the Parish of Witton-le-Wear. His birth was registered at Bishop Auckland in the first three months of 1897. His father Walter Hook, a hewer in the coal mine, was born in North Beechburn in 1869. John's mother, Annie Hook (née Heslop), aged 26, was born at Rough Lee Terrace, Hunwick, in 1875.

Image courtesy of Anita Atkinson

There were seven houses in Stable Row, three of which were occupied by members of the Hook extended family. The three brothers were John Hook, aged 52, and his family, Walter Hook, aged 32, and his family, and Robert Hook, aged 40, and his wife Agnes Hook (née Slee), aged 37, and their five children.

Walter Hook and Annie Heslop , aged 25 and 19 respectively, were married at Bishop Auckland in 1894.
Image courtesy of Myra Griffiths

John and Mary Slee, John Hook's grandparents.

Image courtesy of Myra Griffiths

John Hook had the same great great grandparents as Elizabeth Heslop. She was a school teacher at Howden-le-Wear from at least 1911 to the late 1950s. She taught many generations of Howden-le-Wear village children and will be remembered fondly.
.

Miss Elizabeth Heslop, who taught at Howden-le-Wear Council School, is the lady standing. She was born in 1893 at Hunwick. Mary (sitting) is the eldest, born in 1891. Walter was born in 1897 and Margaret in 1901. This picture was taken around 1911.

Image courtesy of Sue Heslop

In the 1911 census, John Hook was 14 and at school. He now had a sister Nancy, aged 3 years, who had been born in 1908. His father Walter was now a deputy overman in mining. His mother Annie had given birth to four children, but only two, John and Nancy, survived infancy.

Nancy Hook, John's sister, as a baby with cousin Alice Hook who lived next door with parents Agnes and Robert Hook in Park Terrace.

Alice and her husband emigrated to Toronto, Canada, as there was plenty of work on the Canadian Railways.

Image courtesy of Myra Griffiths

John Hook was a pupil at Howden-le-Wear board school. John then attended Wolsingham Grammar School from September 1909 to July 1914. He was originally on a scholarship from the Cuthbert Charity. John was a distinguished all-rounder at school, both in the classroom and on the playing field. His name occurs frequently in the pages of the early Phoenix Magazine, the Wolsingham school magazine that was founded in 1905.

His name is first on the school Honours Board.

1913   John Hook.   1st CL.HONS. Ox. Jun.1

He was eminent as a footballer, cricketer and a runner. Had he survived, he would surely have attained a national reputation. Even while at school, his services as a centre forward were sought by numerous football teams including the league champions. John Hook was only 17 at the time and his modest reply was, 'Wait and see'.

He became a pupil teacher at Wolsingham Grammar School on August 1st 1913 and gained employment on leaving as an assistant master before joining the army. He had been a magnificent scholar, achieving Honours in the Oxford Local Examinations, and had the distinction of achieving the third highest marks in the country at scripture and sixth at maths.

John's family appears to have been deeply involved with the local chapel activities. In a Diamond Jubilee pamphlet published in 1930, it is recorded that "the Great War played havoc with our young men". Five teachers out of the Sunday school were amongst those killed. The Rev. J. W. Collingwood reminisced:

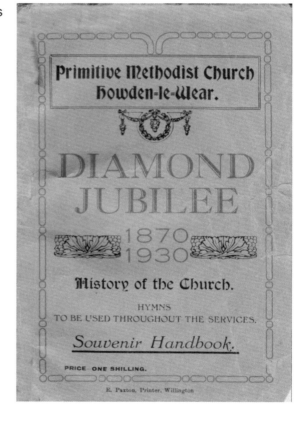

> *"From time to time it was our melancholy duty to visit the relatives of those who had fallen. At Howden-le-Wear the memory of two who fell clearly stands out - clean, Christian, intelligent – Gordon Parkin and John Hook".*

Methodist Church Howden-le-Wear Diamond Jubilee souvenir handbook 1930.

Image courtesy of Joan Potts

John's enlistment document shows he volunteered and enlisted on the 29th February 1916 at the age of 19. His service number was 4823 and he served for the 'Short Service Colours Army Reserve' with the 5th Durham Light Infantry. He had been employed as a school teacher, his height was 5 ft 5 ½ ins and his chest measurement was 35 ½ ins with an expansion of 2 ins.

John was unmarried, did not wish to be vaccinated, and was living with his parents in 3 Park Terrace, Howden-le-Wear. He enlisted as a private and his record shows that on the 7th August 1916 he had been promoted to an 'unpaid acting lance corporal'.

Infantry training at the time would have initially consisted of increasing the enlisted men's physical fitness. In addition they would learn to drill, develop their marching discipline, and undergo essential field craft. Later in the training, a soldier would have specialised to become a rifleman, rifle grenadier, signaller, or bomber etc. Given the large influx of enlisted men in 1916, a huge variety of training facilities were used. These would be in regular camps, but may also include public buildings, church halls, and thousands were billeted in private homes. Later training camps were developed and these could hold thousands of men. As a soldier approaching the time when he would be sent to the front line, he would also be instructed in first aid, gas defence, and other aspects fitting his specific role. Nevertheless, many men arrived totally unprepared at the front line, and they either soon learned or died.

Private Hook was in England until 9th September 1916, at which time he was posted to the British Expeditionary Force in France.

The trenches on the Western Front ran 400 miles from the Belgian coastline to Switzerland. Life in the trenches was an extreme shock for the newly trained troops arriving at the front. After proceeding through the communication trenches the soldiers were faced with a series of front line trenches facing the enemy. Each section was different because it had to meet the specific needs of that particular part of the front, e.g. terrain, nearness of the enemy, how badly damaged it was as a result of previous shelling bombardments etc. Many newcomers felt they could not possibly survive for a few hours, never mind weeks or months. It was usual for the troops to be in the front line for four days, then exchange places with the troops in the reserve trenches behind them, turn and turnabout. Most front line trenches had sand bags placed on the top edge to make a wall facing the enemy. Then there was barbed wire some 20 yards in front of that. The barbed wire consisted of one, two, or three rolls of wire parallel to no-man's-land. On the opposite side, the Germans had similar fortifications.

By their very nature the trenches filled with water, and duck boards were placed in them to try to keep the troops above the water level. Nevertheless, they often stood knee or waist deep in the cold muddy water completely open to the elements. They made dug outs into the sides of the trench and these were roofed with tin sheets with soil heaped on top. This gave them some slight protection and a place to sleep. However, most of the time they slept where they could, often at the side of the trench with their coats pulled up over their heads. In the open trenches they were at the mercy of bombing, snipers, shrapnel, gas attacks, and the elements both day and night.

John had enlisted into 'the poor bloody infantry' and, as such, they had the deadliest role of all and shouldered much of the carrying and labouring work. For long periods the daily routine in the trenches was simply monotonous, but when there was an assault or an attack it reverted to 'a mechanised killing field'. The Durham Light Infantry was an 'Infantry Line Regiment' and had two battalions of 1,000 men each. One would be overseas and the other would be training recruits in the UK. The battalion would be part of a brigade of 5,000 men, and under the command of a division of 20,000 men. Several divisions came under the command of a corps. These corps made up the five Armies the British had in France and Flanders.

In 1916, Private Hook was reported wounded in the fighting and he also suffered a bout of dysentery, from both of which he fully recovered.

Records show that the DLI were involved in the Arras salient, and John would have seen action in the series of eight battles that took place in the spring of 1917: the Battle of Vimy Ridge, the First Battle of Scarpe, the Battle of Bullecourt, the Battle of Lagnicourt and, at the time of his death on the 23rd and 24th of April, the Second Battle of Scarpe.

By late 1916, the High Command of the Allied armies recognised that the war had taken its toll on the front line forces. The casualties from Gallipoli, Somme and Verdun had been high and there was little prospect of victory in sight. Nevertheless, it was planned that there should be a 'joint Spring offensive' in 1917 involving the French and the Russian Armies. The French offensive would be near to Arras and, if successful, this could 'win the war in only 48 hours'.

However, there were a number of strategic problems. The French government desperately needed some success 'to avoid civil unrest' and the morale of their troops was low.   Russia could not meet a commitment for a joint offensive owing to the internal revolutionary factions.

The German army had control of the Vimy Ridge, which dominated the local area, and had reinforced their lines on the Arras salient and General Haig would rather have seen the major offensive in the north around the Ypres area. This meant that it would be a 'French only offensive' and reluctantly General Haig, overruled by Lloyd George the Prime Minister, agreed to commit troops in support of the French.

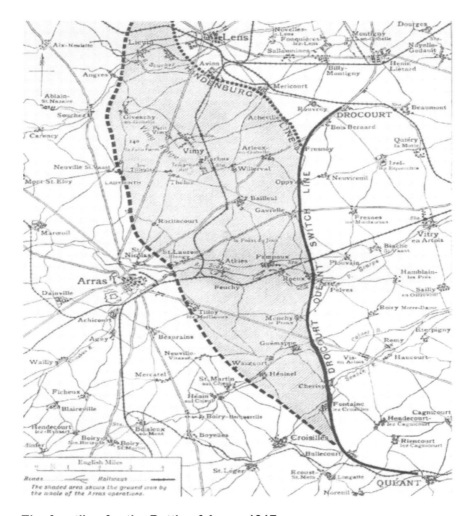

The frontline for the Battle of Arras, 1917.

Image courtesy of www.1914-1918.net

At Arras, the Allies had the 1st, 3rd and 5th armies under Generals Horne, Allenby and Gough respectively. Allenby's 3rd Army included battalions from the DLI. They were opposed by the German Sixth Army under General Von Falkenhausen. The Germans had developed a new strategy called the 'elastic defence', in that they had some seven divisions held in reserve. This new strategy saw their front line troops retreat to heavily fortified defensive positions. When the attack from the Allies had ceased to make progress, the Germans would commit reserve troops into the field by way of counterattack. For nine months the Germans, with the use of Russian prisoners, had built some 'fearsome defensive features' as the British called the 'Hindenburg Line'. By 18th March 1917 the Germans had withdrawn behind this line, and this posed significant problems for the Allied offensive. For French Commander Nivelle, it saw the forthcoming attack being pitched against a 'salient that no longer existed'.

Nevertheless, the planned offensive went ahead as agreed. The British started their operations a few days before those of the French in order to draw the Germans' reserve troops to the North. Some 12 miles of tunnelling had been undertaken in the area. The work had been carried out by southern hemisphere troops and 'bantams' from Northern England mining regions. The underground workings were capable of hiding some 24,000 troops and, being well lit, contained kitchens, latrines, medical stations and a fully equipped operating theatre. These would enable the troops to arrive on the battlefield in secrecy and safety. A preliminary Allied barrage began on 20th March 1917 on a 24 mile front. Some 2,689,000 shells were fired, 1,000,000 more than used at the Battle of the Somme. The Battle of Arras was divided into 8 sections and the Second Battle of Scarpe was the fifth phase.

Zero hour was delayed for a day and the attack began at 5.30am on 9th April 1917. It was preceded by a 'hurricane bombardment' lasting five minutes. When the day came it was snowing heavily and the advance across 'no-man's-land' was hindered by snow drifts.

The German casualties were not heavy but the troops were exhausted. They had had to keep the dugout entrances open, were demoralised by the lack of rations, and the inability to cook their food owing to the continual bombardment. Some troops had not eaten for three days. To add to the misery of the Germans, over the previous ten hours gas shells had been used. The combination of the unusual bombardment, snow and poor visibility saw German troops being caught unawares and many were taken prisoner. Only half-dressed, others tried to escape and, as a result, the first two trenches were taken. One reason for the Allied initial success was that General Luddendorf's reserve troops had been held too far back from the front line and they were unable to arrive to counter attack on the 10th and 11th April.

Troops at the Second Battle of the Scarpe in 1917, often called the most savage infantry battle of WWI.

Image courtesy of www.1914-1918.net

The Second Battle of Scarpe started on 23rd April and involved the DLI. Therefore it is likely that John Hook would have been present during this battle. The assault began on the enemy positions which ran south of Vis an Atrois to Guemappe crossroads. Promptly on that morning at 4.45am, eighty four 18 pounders and thirty Howitzers began to bomb the enemy positions. However, this drew heavy counter fire and caused numerous casualties amongst the men huddled in the assembly trenches. Nonetheless, the two spearhead battalions had 'gone over the bags' but within a hundred yards they had run into their own 'creeping barrage' and this caused many casualties. Nevertheless, they reached their objectives by 5.25am and began to consolidate their positions. Later in the day, the Germans counter attacked and, in order to stop the forward troops of the 150th Brigade being decimated, the exhausted attackers were forced back into their original starting position by 11.30am.

Reports at the time state that Private John Hook suffered a wound to his thigh and it was bound by members of the Royal Army Medical Corps (RAMC). Before passing on they had instructed him to return to the safety of the rear. He refused and insisted on staying with some others whose condition made their removal impossible.

Wounded soldiers were usually assessed by the RAMC as falling into three categories: a minor wound, hopeless case, and severe but survivable. It appears that when John was found by the medical corps his wounds were 'treatable' and, if he had returned to safety, he could have survived. When the stretcher bearers were brought up later John was found dead. He died in action in France on the 23rd April, 1917, at the age of 20. For some reason his body was not recovered and he is remembered on the Arras War Memorial in Bay 8.

On 14th May 1915, the 1st/5th Battalion DLI became part of the 150th Brigade and was incorporated into the 50th Northumberland Division.

That afternoon General Allenby sent a telegram to say 'the blue line must be taken that day at all costs'. Although the four battalions of the 150th Brigade could barely muster a full battalion between them, the attack was renewed. The artillery laid on a creeping barrage similar to the morning but this time:

> *'due to the steadiness and determination of the advance it proved too much for the enemy.....beaten by the long slogging match.... parties surrendered freely while others retreated under fire'.*
> *(From '1917 At all Costs Monchy Le Preux')*

Private John Hook is remembered on the Howden-le-Wear War Memorial. His name was inscribed on the Honoured Memory Board to the Old Boys at Wolsingham School, as well as having a memorial oak tree planted in his memory to grow in the school grounds.

John Hook's memorial oak tree at Wolsingham Grammar School.
Image courtesy of Kathleen Parkin

John's Heslop grandparents had a substantial memorial erected in Hunwick graveyard to John and the other members of their family who died in action during the Great War. Not only did they lose their grandson John Hook, they also lost their son-in-law William Carter who was killed in northern Italy on the 5th December 1917, aged 35, and was buried in Giavera British Cemetery. Their third loss was their son John G. Heslop who 'fell in action' in Italy on the 28th March 1918. His body was never recovered and he is remembered on the Pozieres Memorial near Albert. The family would be in deep mourning for their three lost soldiers.

The family memorial at Hunwick graveyard.

Image courtesy of Kathleen Parkin

John Hook's parents Walter and Annie and his sister Nancy continued to live at Park Terrace (Stable Row) for the rest of their lives. They appear to have moved into other houses in the terrace, ending up at number 7. John's sister Nancy married John Clough and had no children. John Clough was a reporter for the Northern Echo and Nancy worked from home as an elocution teacher until her death.

John Hook's war medals did not pass on to either the Hook or the Heslop extended family, but to John Clough's sister and her family, even though there were still Hook and Heslop family members living in the locality.

Henry Walker

The name F. Walker appears on the Howden-le-Wear War Memorial. It has been difficult to pinpoint F. Walker, but the following soldier seems likely to be the soldier listed.

In 1901, a Walker family lived at Blackett's Yard, 111 Wheatbottom, Crook, in County Durham.

John Nicholas Walker was the head of the house and was aged 29 years. His wife was Caroline (née Hardman), aged 26, years and had married John at Bishop Auckland Registry Office on the 1st June 1891 at the age of 16. John and Caroline had four children: Frederick William born in 1895, Henry born in1897, Emily born in1898 and John Thomas born in 1900.

By 1910 the family was living at 21 Valley Terrace, Howden-le-Wear, and twins George and Nora were born, but their mother Caroline died on the 11th December around the time of the children's birth.

The 1911 Census shows that John, now a widower, continued to live with his family of six children in their four roomed house at Valley Terrace. John and his two eldest sons, Frederick, now aged 16, and Henry, aged 14, worked in the local coal mining industry. Henry must have started work at 14 years of age.

Happily for John, he married for a second time on the 13th June 1913 to Florence Todd from Crook.

During 1914 and 1915, both his sons Frederick William and Henry enlisted in the Durham Light Infantry. Frederick Walker, Private 250096, served in the 1st/6th Battalion, survived the war, returned home and lived at 5 The Bungalows, Foundry Fields, Crook, where he died aged 67 on 12th January 1962. However, Henry Walker, Private 24776, served in the 15th Battalion and was killed in action, aged 21 years, in Flanders on 3rd May 1917. His name is inscribed on the Arras Memorial in France.

It is highly possible that Henry was the soldier from Howden-le-Wear remembered on the village War Memorial. The initial on the War Memorial is F. Walker while the initial on the Church Roll of Honour is W. Walker. Private F. W. Walker was from Howden-le-Wear and served in the DLI, but survived. However, his brother Private H. Walker, also from Howden-le-Wear, served in the DLI and died in action, but there is no H. Walker on the Memorial. It is reasonable to assume that somehow the brothers' names have been mixed up, but difficult to be sure as no member of the family has come forward to try to rectify the error.

Sydney Luck

Sidney Harold Luck was born in Howden-le-Wear, and lived at High Street, Church Street and at Low Beechburn. He was the son of Septimus and Mary Jane Luck and his baptism was held at the Wesleyan Methodist Chapel in Willington on April 18th 1895.

According to the 1911 Census, Sydney was one of fifteen children, although, by that year, six of his siblings had died. As a young man he worked in a brickyard and was later a miner, as were many of the men in his family.

Within weeks of Britain's involvement in the war, Sidney Luck, aged 19 years and 4 months, joined the many who agreed to serve King and Country. Private 20341 Luck joined the 15th Battalion, the Durham Light Infantry. He was a single man, described as small in stature and with brown hair and blue eyes. As part of the Expeditionary Force to France, he left England in September 1915 only to return two months later suffering from a gunshot wound to his foot. In February 1916, Sydney returned to the front line in France. He did have two weeks' home leave in Howden-le-Wear early in 1917 and returned to France on the 17th March 1917. Sydney rejoined his unit and just seven weeks later, in early May, he was killed in action.

At this time, the battalion was fighting during the Battle of Arras. The weather was very hot and humid during the first week of May, and the 15th DLI were in trenches so close to the enemy lines that, when they were being shelled by British heavy Howitzers, the British troops were withdrawn from the front lines. When the British did attack the enemy, they suffered many casualties. This was not helped by the one hour delay in the expected tank support, which caused major attack problems.

Fighting under the hot sun for long periods left the British soldiers exhausted and eventually, late in the afternoon, they were relieved. On the 5th May, 68 men were wounded and 28 were pronounced as missing, one of whom was Sydney Luck.

On the morning of the 6th May, movement was seen in a shell hole not more than 40 yards from the German front line. A wounded man was waving his water bottle. Sending out a stretcher party in daylight was impossible, but Private Michael Heavyside of the 15th DLI volunteered to take out food and water. Miraculously he reached the survivor unharmed. He helped the injured man, who had been without food and water for several days, and then crawled back under night cover and went with the stretcher party to bring the soldier back to allied lines. For this brave action he was awarded the Victoria Cross. Private Heaviside and Private Luck, both Durham miners, would have fought together for several years and would be known to each other.

Sydney Luck was one of the missing and his body was never recovered. His death is commemorated on the Arras Memorial alongside the names of 35,000 servicemen of different nationalities who have no known grave.

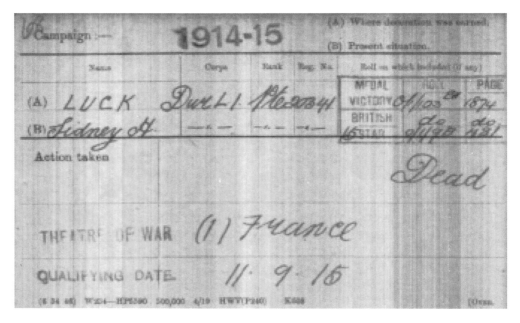

Private Sydney Luck's Medal Roll Card showing the award of the 1915 Star, British and Victory Medals.

Image courtesy of www.ancestry.co.uk

All servicemen were advised to write a will prior to seeing action and a brief sentence in Private Luck's service record dated March 15th 1917 states that, in the event of his death, the whole of his property and effects were to be given to his Mother, Mary Jane Luck, of 44 Low Beechburn, Crook.

In September of the same year, almost three years after the day of his attestation, his Mother received her son's belongings: 2 razors, a cap badge, pocket book, 2 buttons, 2 religious pamphlets, a pocket case, photos, gold stripe, coins, a pipe, cigarette case, mirror, card, scissors and 2 Gospels of St. Luke. This was a small testimony to his short life of 22 years.

Thomas Horn

Thomas Edward Horn was born in Middleton-in-Teesdale in County Durham in 1891, his birth having been registered in the last quarter of that year. His father, Thomas, a stone quarryman, was also born in Middleton-in-Teesdale, and his mother, Alice, 15 years younger than her husband, was born in Northallerton, North Yorkshire. The family lived at 40 Market Place, Middleton-in-Teesdale. Thomas Edward was the second child, having an older sister, Mary, born in 1890.

At the time of the 1901 Census, the family was still living at 40 Market Place, Middleton-in-Teesdale. Thomas, aged 9, now had two younger sisters, Mabel, aged 5, and Ethel, aged 3. A younger brother, Sidney, born in 1893, had died in infancy, and was buried on the 21st November 1893, only five days after his baptism.

At the time of the 1911 Census, Thomas Edward was living with his widowed mother Alice and his two younger sisters Ethel and Beatrice and younger brother Joshua at The Hollow, Low Beechburn, between Howden-le-Wear and Crook. His father had died in 1906. Thomas Edward was shown as a putter, working in a local coal mine.

Private Thomas Horn enlisted in the Durham Light Infantry but later transferred to the 13th Northumberland Fusiliers, probably about the time he married Mary Brewis in Morpeth in the summer of 1915. Mary and Thomas did not have long together as he was soon posted overseas to Flanders and died on the 16th June 1917. He is remembered on the Arras Memorial as he was one of the missing soldiers whose body was never recovered.

His name is also inscribed on the Howden-le-Wear War Memorial.

UK, Soldiers Died in the Great War, 1914-1919 about Thomas Edward Horn

Name:	**Thomas Edward Horn**
Birth Place:	Middleton-in-teesdale, Durham
Death Date:	16 Jun 1917
Death Place:	France and Flanders
Enlistment Place:	Bishop Auckland, Durham
Rank:	Private
Regiment:	Northumberland Fusiliers
Battalion:	13th Battalion
Regimental Number:	35349
Type of Casualty:	Died
Theatre of War:	Western European Theatre
Comments:	Formerly 3644, Durham L.I.
Other Records:	**Search for 'Thomas Edward Horn' in other WWI collections**

Save This Record
Attach this record to a person in your tree as a source record, or save for later evaluation.

Save ☐

Source Information:
Military-Genealogy.com, comp. *UK, Soldiers Died in the Great War, 1914-1919* [database on-line]. Provo, UT, USA: Ancestry.com Operations Inc, 2008.
Original data: *British and Irish Military Databases*. The Naval and Military Press Ltd.

Description:
This database contains information extracted from 81 volumes of soldiers that died in World War I. It includes over 703,000 individuals. Information listed may include: name of soldier, birthplace, enlistment place, residence, number, decoration, rank, regiment, battalion, type of casualty, death date, death place, and theater of war served in. Learn more...

Extract from the Soldiers Who Died in the Great War 1914-1919 database with the details of Thomas Horn.

Thomas Evans

Thomas Evans was born in Crook, in County Durham, about 1880. His father, John, a coal miner, was originally from Staffordshire, whilst his mother, Dorothy, was born farther up the Wear Valley. He had two older sisters, Annie and Elizabeth, and an older brother, William. The family lived at Dawson Street in Crook.

The 1891 Census shows that the family was living at Welsh Row in Crook, and Thomas had two younger brothers, Joseph and John.

By the time of the 1901 Census, Thomas was living in Gateshead, and is shown as a castman in the coal industry. He was married to Sarah, with a 10 month old son, and also living with him were his mother-in-law, brother-in-law and two sisters-in-law.

The 1911 Census shows Thomas working as a coal miner hewer living with his wife and sons James and John, aged 11 and 6 respectively, at 14 Athol Street, Dunston, on the south bank of the River Tyne. By the time of the war, however, he had returned to his native region of County Durham, and was living in Victoria Cottages in Howden-le-Wear. He was working at Bowden Close Colliery at nearby Helmington Row, before he enlisted in the Durham Light Infantry.

It is interesting to break for a moment to look at the history of Thomas Evans' mother, Dorothy. By 1901 she was widowed, and was living at Church Hill, Helmington Row, with her two other sons. She was an agricultural worker. Her son Joseph, now 16, was a putter, working below ground, and son John, now 11 (although the transcript shows him as 14, which is inaccurate) was a fire clay worker at a local brickworks.

At the time of the 1911 Census, she was still living at Church Hill in Helmington Row, but was now running a boarding house. One son, John, was still living with her, and he was a coal miner hewer.

We may speculate what factors prompted Thomas to return to his native area of County Durham. His mother was now widowed, and he had two brothers who were miners. It was entirely possible that they were working at Bowden Close Colliery, where he was to work. Could these factors in any way have influenced his decision to return to the area?

Thomas enlisted in the 12th DLI with the Regimental Number 270055 (previously 3999). The 12th (Service) Battalion was originally formed at Newcastle in September 1914, and moved around various barracks in the south of England before being mobilised for war, landing at Boulogne on the

26th August 1915. Thomas arrived in France on the 27th October 1915 and was soon engaged in heavy fighting.

The following year the 12th DLI took part in various actions on the Western Front as part of the 20th and 27th Divisions. The next year, the battalion saw further action, including the German attack on Vimy Ridge. In 1917, the 12th DLI took part in the Battle of Messines, and the First and Second Battles of Passchendaele. During one of these Battles, Private Thomas Evans was awarded the Military Medal for extreme gallantry.

On the 4th July1917, the battalion, including Private Evans, paraded before the King along the La Clytte-Reninghelst Road. He may even have been awarded his Military Medal by the King on this occasion.

On the 10th July they went back into front line trenches near Klein Zillebeke, where the Germans were entrenched in very superior concrete shelters. Two officers and forty men from the 12th DLI rushed a German pillbox round which a box barrage had been placed. Both officers were wounded and there was some very fierce fighting, but five German soldiers were captured. Three of the Durham men did not return, despite one of the officers having gone back to look for them. One of these men was Private Thomas Evans from Howden-le-Wear.

It is unclear whether or not his body was recovered, but Private Evans is remembered in Oxford Road Cemetery, near Ypres. The *Auckland Chronicle* of the 2nd August had the following announcement:

> **'Fallen in France**
>
> *Mrs Evans, of Victoria Cottages, Howden-le-Wear, received the sad news on Saturday that her husband, Pte Thomas Evans, 12th DLI, had fallen in action "somewhere in France". This brave soldier had taken part in a good deal of hard fighting and some time ago was recommended for the D.C. Medal. In a letter to Mrs Evans, one of his officers spoke of Pte Evans as a brave, courageous, painstaking soldier. Previous to his enlistment he was employed by Messrs Pease and Partners at Bowden Close Colliery. Great sympathy is extended to the sorrowing family.'*

A Memorial Service was held in St Mary's Church in Howden-le-Wear in mid-August 1917 to remember two of their young men who would not be coming home.

> *'A large congregation of sympathetic mourners attended the Howden-le-Wear Parish Church on Sunday morning when a service*

was held in memory of the late Pte T. Evans and Pte D. Etherington who have both fallen in action. The Vicar, the Rev. B. S. Spencer, preached an appropriate sermon and made touching reference to the fallen heroes, and gave words of comfort to the bereaved. Mr May, the organist, played the Dead March.'

From *Auckland Chronicle*, 2rd August, 1917.

David Etherington

David Etherington was born in 1892 in Howden-le-Wear. His parents were John and Rebecca Etherington who moved to Railway Street after living at Penshaw in County Durham. David was the eighth of nine children and his mother died in 1899, aged 43. When the 1901 Census was taken, John Etherington and six of his children were living in Railway Street, Howden-le-Wear.

The 1911 Census shows that David, aged 18, and his brother Robert, aged 26, were boarding with Thomas and Mary Halliburton at Howden-le-Wear. David was working as a putter boy in the mines and Robert as a brick maker's apprentice.

Private David Etherington enlisted in the Army in Sunderland. His Medal Roll Card indicates that he left Britain for overseas service in the Middle East on the 14th November 1915. He served as a Trooper in the 14th King's Hussars Battalion with the Household Cavalry and the Cavalry of the Line. His regimental number was 7435. The regiment had been serving in India and were posted directly to Mesopotamia in 1915 where they stayed until May 1918.

The conditions for the British soldiers in Mesopotamia were horrendous. With temperatures over 120 degrees Fahrenheit being common, arid desert and regular storms causing floods, flies and mosquitoes led to appalling levels of sickness and death through disease. Units found they were short of officers and all too often reinforcements were poorly trained and ill equipped for the conditions. The medical care was poor, with wounded men spending up to two weeks on boats before reaching hospital. During the four years of fighting in the Mesopotamian campaign, more than 31,000 officers and men from the British and Indian armies died in combat or from disease in what was a little known theatre of war.

The infrastructure of Mesopotamia was poor, there were very few roads and all mobility was by boats on the Rivers Tigris and Euphrates. The oil reserves were essential for British ships and early in the war they placed an occupying force to protect the pipelines from Basra. Battles occurred during 1915 and 1916 around Basra and as far north as Baghdad until the British surrendered the garrison at Kut-al-Amara in April 1916. This was a blow to the British but a real boost to the Turkish morale. New command structures were established by the British and eventually they managed to push the Turks back. By the end of 1917 and the beginning of 1918, the British and Russian forces were attacking from the north and from Palestine and, with the British in the south, the Turkish army was defeated.

David would certainly have seen some very hard fighting and experienced very difficult living conditions during his two and a half years in the Middle East. He died on the 21st July 1917 in Baghdad. There was no recorded fighting taking place at that time. It is probable that he died from his wounds or disease. He was buried in the Baghdad North Gate War Cemetery and was later awarded the British War Medal, the Victory Medal and the 1915 Star.

The *Auckland Chronicle* of Thursday 23rd August 1917 reported that a Memorial Service was held in the Parish Church, Howden-le-Wear, on the previous Sunday morning for two of its own, David Etherington and Thomas Evans. A sad day for the village!

Jonathan Bell

Jonathan William Bell was born in the spring of 1898. The 1901 Census shows the Bell family living at Church Street, Howden-le-Wear, and at home was his mother Margaret with eight children ranging in age from 15 years to 2 months. Jonathon was the sixth child. His father, Richard, must have been away from home on the night of the Census as his location has not been traced.

By the time of the 1911 Census, the family was living at 43 The Leazes, Throckley, Newburn, near Newcastle. Father Richard and three of his sons were miners and Jonathon was employed as a brick factory labourer.

Private Jonathon Bell enlisted in the army at Bishop Auckland, and served as a Private in the 1st/5th Battalion of the Prince of Wales' Own West Yorkshire Regiment. His service number was 235619. He had previously served with the 6th Durham Light Infantry, service number 74390. It is not known when he went to France, but he would have seen some fierce fighting. The war diary for the 1st/5th Battalion of the Prince of Wales' Own

West Yorkshire Regiment paints a vivid picture of events of the 7th to 10th October 1917, the time when Jonathon was killed.

The battalion were entrenched near the Passchendaele Ridge at Wieltje. During the 7th and 8th of October, they suffered some minor shelling but no casualties or damage. On the night of the 8th they experienced some very heavy rain and were preparing for an attack on the 9th October. The night was very dark and they had great difficulty traversing the mud.

The assembly position was reached and the battalion was in position for the attack about 1.20am. They waited until 5.20am when they advanced behind the artillery barrage. The ground was extremely wet and cut up and great difficulty was experienced keeping pace with the barrage, especially crossing the Stroombeek, which was a small stream and marsh land about 200 yards wide.

The enemy barrage retaliated and fell heavily on the Stroombeck and behind the assembly position. Few casualties were caused by the barrage but the battalion came under machine gun and sniper fire. The battle continued throughout the rest of the day and on through the following day with a number of commanding officers being killed and replaced. The battalion went on to attack the lower slopes of the Passchendaele Ridge. During these two days of battle, the battalion suffered the following casualties: 4 officers and 48 other ranks killed, 8 officers and 182 other ranks wounded, and 2 officers and 56 other ranks declared missing. Jonathon was killed during the fighting on the 9th October and he was buried at Zonnebeke, in Belgium. He was only 20 years of age, but this was one of the horrendous battles of the war. It is difficult to imagine the conditions experienced with the mud, shelling and continuous noise, and men dying all around.

Jonathon's older brother, John Everitt Thompson Bell, was a coal miner/driver before the war and he also enlisted and was posted to the Royal Field Artillery in September 1914 at the age of 19 years and 6 months. He was 5 ft 5 ins tall. He was promoted quickly to sergeant in August 1915 and went to Flanders in November 1915. He was given leave home in June 1916 and again in July 1917. He came back to England in October 1917 and then went back to France on the 16th January 1918. John was awarded the Belgian Croix de Guerre for bravery on the battlefield following events in August 1918.

John saw much action but survived and was discharged from the services in January 1919 after serving 5 years and 211 days before the colours.

Randolph Gordon Parkin

Randolph Gordon Parkin was born in 1896 and christened at Crook Primitive Methodist Chapel on 15th October of that year. To his family and friends he was known by his middle name, Gordon.

The 1891 census records the Parkin family living at Hargill Road in Howden-le-Wear, and the head of the household was Gordon's grandfather, William Parkin, aged 47. He was married to Annie, aged 38, and was working as a coal miner. They had six children, the eldest being Gordon's father George. He was aged 18 and was also employed as a coal miner. There was also Sarah Hannah, aged 15, who is recorded as being a 'school teacher'. The four younger children were William, aged 13, Edward, aged 10, Joseph, aged 8, and Charles, aged 6, all of whom were in education. In addition to the family members, they also had a 'boarder' called Edward Chegwin, aged 24, who was also a coal miner.

The 1901 census identifies the family living in 54 High Street, North Bedburn, near Howden-le-Wear. As head of the household, George was described as a 'travelling draper'. Boarding with the family at that time was Lena Pallister, a 17 year old domestic servant who was born at Witton Park.

The 1911 census shows Gordon as living with his parents George, now aged 38, and Mary Hannah Parkin, now aged 37, in Denver House, Howden-le-Wear. Gordon was their eldest son, aged 14. He had a younger brother called Joseph William, aged 11, and younger sisters called Annie May, aged 8, and Lena, aged 3. They no longer had the domestic servant identified in the 1901 census, and Gordon's father now described himself as an independent draper. Given that Gordon was employed as a 'shop assistant' it could be presumed he was working for this father, possibly at their home address of Denver House at the bottom of Rumby Hill, Howden.

The family history shows that the Parkin family was deeply involved with the local Methodist Church and, as such, they believed it was their Christian duty to 'serve the community'. As identified in their business advertisement, they felt:

'Service is the Golden Key....service is the way all men must tread. Service is the justification of your existence, our existence and service is our hope and aim in life.'

Therefore it is evident that the Parkin family believed it was their duty to serve the community through God – and for Gordon this included service to his 'King and Country'.

If we consider the Parkin family history, it identifies how much they had prospered following the 1881 census which records William Parkin as being a 'coal miner'. By 1930, they had established themselves as independent drapers and tailors owning a warehouse business.

They not only had a shop in Howden-le-Wear but had one at 65a Blackett Street, Newcastle.

Parkin's shop is in the foreground of the photograph of High Street, Howden-le-Wear.

Image courtesy of Howden-le-Wear History Society

MRS. ANNIE PARKIN, SENR.,
One of the pioneers of 60 years ago,
is now a Class Leader.

MRS G. PARKIN,
Takes a hand in everything.

MR. GEORGE PARKIN,
A Sunday School Scholar, Teacher, Society Steward, Sunday School
Superintendent, Leader, Treasurer to Trust.

MR. REDVERS PARKIN,
Sunday School Scholar, Teacher,
Now Secretary to the Trust.

MISS A. M. PARKIN,
Sunday School Scholar, Teacher,
Now Church Organist.

Gordon Parkin's family held posts within Howden-le-Wear Methodist
Church and it shows photographs of Gordon's mother, Mrs G. Parkin,
and his sister, Annie May.

Gordon's father George is identified in the Methodist Diamond Jubilee pamphlet as a 'leader of the church'. It also refers to:

> *'A walk and talk with Gordon Parkin when he was home on leave. That brave young Christian was one of the finest products of the Church'.*

It also records that the Great War played havoc with their young men, as five teachers out of the Sunday School were amongst those killed.

The Rev. J. W. Collingwood reminisced:

> *'From time to time it was our melancholy duty to visit the relatives of those who had fallen. At Howden-le-Wear the memory of two who fell clearly stands out – clean, Christian, intelligent – Gordon Parkin and John Hook'.*

The booklet also refers to the history of the chapel. In 1930:

> *'as far as is known there are only four people alive today who were connected with our church when it was erected in 1870 ... Mrs Annie Parkin senior, who still resides in the village ... she had attended the meetings when they were held in Mr Head's house....she helped with the first sewing meetings, being a dressmaker herself, ...helped with all the teas, and was a member of the first Choir'.*

Gordon was 18 years old when war was declared in August 1914. The British Expeditionary Force had been formed and had left for Europe to support their allies in Belgium and France. At this time volunteers were asked for and many joined the local Pals' Brigades, where they were promised they would serve alongside friends, neighbours and work colleagues. The feeling at this time was that young men should hurry up to enlist as it would all be over by Christmas. However, by 1916, it was evident that more troops were required and that legislation was needed to bolster the armed forces on all fronts of the war.

The Enlisting Military Service Act came into force on 27th January 1916 and all males between the ages of 19 and 41 years were eligible for conscription. At this time Gordon would have been 20 years old and would have been directly affected by this legislation. By the 25th May 1916 the age of conscription was brought down to 18 years and all married men became eligible. There were a number of jobs that were 'protected' like mining etc. but that would not have applied to Gordon. By this time, there was no choice into which service, regiment or unit an enlisted soldier would be drafted.

Gordon enlisted at Bishop Auckland and was conscripted into the Royal Horse Artillery and a period of training followed. He would have been sent to an 'artillery training camp' which may have been at Newcastle, or he may have gone further afield to 'instruction batteries' at Shoeburyness, or Larkhill. The role of the artillery was to provide bombardments in support of the front line troops in the trenches and during their manoeuvres.

For Gordon the artillery training would have been both technical and demanding. The artillery units, both heavy and light, had become crucial in making advances, or maintaining the defensive positions. However, when Gordon began his training there was an extreme shortage of guns and shells, and very few ranges available where live rounds could be used.

As WWI progressed the Royal Horse Artillery's role changed to meet the demands of the trench warfare. By 1916, the role of the Royal Horse Artillery was modified with the result that light artillery units were now 'embedded into the infantry units in the front line'. This would have seen Gordon's unit becoming part of the Royal Field Artillery rather than being a separate supporting unit and the light artillery came under joint command. This was in order better to co-ordinate the needs of the artillery and the infantry. However, it also brought the gun batteries nearer to the front line and in doing so increased the danger of attracting direct enemy fire. Counter bombardments targeted the flashes as the enemy guns fired, and a crucial part of any encounter in trench warfare was to eliminate the enemy gun batteries.

The main source of transport for all the armies was based on horse power, with motorised vehicles being used more and more as the war progressed. The horse carriages would haul the guns backwards and forwards along the front line. A typical light artillery battery would consist of six crew members, six limbered horses and they would move the Howitzers or mortars into position where they could support the infantry in the front line. Different types of shells were used for specific purposes: to bombard the front line so as to weaken the defensive trenches of the Germans; to cut wires at night in readiness for an assault the next day; to shell specific targets, such as the German batteries; and to fire gas shells when the weather (wind) conditions were favourable.

Artillery being transported across the battlefield on the Western Front. A typical battery crew could fire some 4.5 Howitzer shells at the rate of about four rounds per minute. This could see them firing some 800 to 1,000 rounds per day.

Image courtesy of www.1914-1918.net

Gordon was present at Passchendaele in September and October 1917. He was assigned to the "D" Howitzer Battery of the 102nd Field Artillery Brigade, which was part of the 23rd Division of the 2nd Army. This would have seen him positioned to take part on the assault on Passchendaele, some 12 kilometres north west of Ypres.

By the end of 1916, the British High Command decided that a major push was needed to end the stalemate on the Western Front. It was decided that an advance on the Ypres salient in Belgium was needed. This was to stop the German access to Belgian ports for naval and submarine warfare, and to capture the strategically important railhead of Roulers. If successful, it could also prove to be a decisive factor in winning the war.

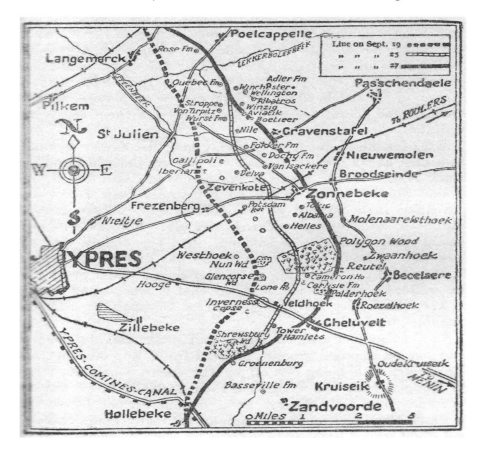

Image courtesy of www.1914-1918. net

In preparation for this attack, the 2nd and 5th British Armies, consisting of some 150,000 men each, joined with the French First Army along an 18 kilometre front in the Passchendaele area. In addition, they were supported by Corps from the Australian and Canadian armies. In preparation, the 2nd Army's heavy artillery increased from 112 guns to 575 and the light artillery guns rose from 210 to 720.

Haig's battle formation saw him place the French First Army on the north flank of the salient, General Gough's 5th Army in the centre, and General Plumer's 2nd Army to the south. The opposing force was the German Fourth Army commanded by General Friedrich Bertram Sixt Von Armin.

British soldiers carrying a wounded colleague through the mud to the first aid post. *Image courtesy of www.1914-1918.net*

Soldiers waiting to board a Red Cross train.
Image courtesy of www.1914-1918.net

The Passchendaele Offensive became known as the 3rd Battle of Ypres and it started on the 17th July 1917. Some 19 tunnels had been dug under the German lines and they were detonated at 3.10am. The massive explosions were heard as far away as London and were the precursor to the attack. Although these initial explosions decimated the German defences, they did not produce the 'final breakthrough' that Haig had expected. As a result, although gains were made, the German lines held firm and the trench warfare continued throughout July and August.

By this time, the war had been fought for over two years, and the Allied field artillery had developed a new approach in their use of artillery during attacks on the German lines. Previously the heavy and light artillery had bombarded the enemy trenches for days, weeks or months prior to an advance. Over the course of the war it became very evident that the Germans were very well dug into their trenches and, as soon as the barrage stopped, they would rise out of their bunkers in time to catch the advancing troops in no-man's-land. Struggling through the wire, mud, shell holes, smoke and shell fire, the advancing infantry would often be 'cut down' before they reached even their first battle plan objective.

At the Battle of the Somme the first day saw some 60,000 allied casualties. In the light of this, the Royal Field Artillery was embedded into the front line units and a 'creeping barrage' provided a curtain of fire just in front of the advancing troops. With careful planning between the infantry and the artillery commanders a 'rule of thumb' saw the barrage moving forward at about 50 metres per minute once the offensive had begun. This strategy needed close cooperation between the advancing troops and the supporting field artillery, or the artillery would be killing their own advancing troops. What it also did was place the light artillery nearer to the front line and, in doing so, they became increasingly exposed to enemy counter fire. Although the creeping barrage was effective, it saw advances on a 'bite and hold' basis, and as such could not provide the decisive breakthrough on a wide front that General Haig was seeking.

By September 1917, army records report that the 23rd Division, consisting of mainly North Country troops, and part of Plumer's 2nd Army were heavily engaged in action. On the 19th/20th September they had 'carried Inverness Copse' and after a counterattack in the neighbourhood of Dumbarton Lakes captured Veldhoek and the line of their final objective some 500 yards further east.

By early October they were near Broodseinde. General Haig's Despatches record that the 23rd Division repulsed German attacks with 'great loss of life' and say about the artillery:

> 'As our infantry advanced our guns had to follow at the cost of incredible exertion ...for the most part destitute of cover and directly overlooked by the enemy. It would be easy to multiply the instances

of individual courage... and when a signal for urgent artillery support was given at the same moment as a gas attack our gunners have thrown aside their gas masks with the full knowledge of the consequences ....until the enemy attack was fought off'.

The record states that Randolph Gordon Parkin, Regimental Number 127230, Acting Bombardier in the "D" Battery (Howitzers), died on the 14th October 1917. The research, however, did not give the actual circumstances of his death. It did not identify exactly where and when he was wounded, what his actual injuries were, or how long he survived them.

It could be that, as the weather at this time in early October saw *'squalls of cold drenching rain.....that came down in torrents',* he may have died of exposure where he fell.

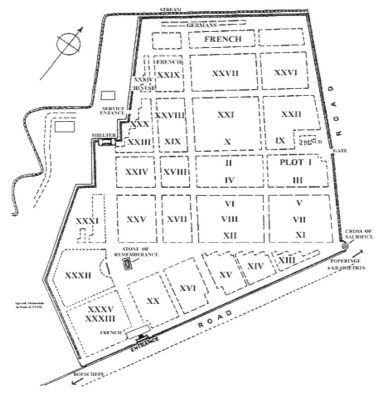

LIJSSENTHOEK MILITARY CEMETERY

Image courtesy of www.cwgc.org

Gordon was buried at Lijssenhoek Cemetery near Ypres in grave XX1 C7. Lijssenhoek was positioned on the main communication line between the front and the Allied Military bases. Gordon was later awarded the Victory Medal and the British Medal.

Thomas Robinson

Thomas William Robinson was born 1897 in the Gate House, Commercial Street, Crook, and was the eldest child of John and Hannah Robinson. Soon afterwards the family moved to 17 Woodifield Row, Crook, where Elizabeth Hannah was born in 1902, Alfred in 1905 and Alice during the winter of 1907.

On the 30th October 1907, John, aged 35, was working as a hewer at Woodifield Colliery.   He was levering a piece of stone down with a 4 ft plate and the stone fell suddenly striking him on the chest. Nine months later, John died on 5th June 1908, from a clot of blood in the windpipe.

Woodifield Colliery was owned by Balckow and Vaughan Company Ltd, who also owned Fir Tree Colliery, and young Thomas was given a job as a pit pony driver as soon as he was able to leave school.

The 1911 Census shows the family living in a miner's house at Loves Beechburn with the head of the house being Hannah, a 35 year old widow, and Thomas, aged 14, the only wage earner, a pit pony driver. Elizabeth and Alfred were at school and Alice was at home with her mother.

Private Thomas Robinson attested with the 6th Durham Light Infantry, Number 2621, on the 28th September 1914 at the age of 17 years and 10 months. He was 5 ft 3 ins tall and weighed 132 lbs. His development was fair and he had good eyesight. His occupation was as a Durham miner. His home at that time was 5 Chapel Row, Greenhead, and he was still living with his mother.

On the 23rd November 1915, Thomas was training in Newcastle and was admitted to Bensham Hospital with scabies, a common complaint of the time. After reaching his 19th birthday, Thomas was sent to France on the 20th July 1916, and on the 5th September he transferred to the Loyal North Lancashire Regiment and was given the number 26566.

Thomas served in the trenches and on the 4th December he was admitted to the hospital for one night with influenza. On the 16th December he was readmitted with myalgia and pneumonia at Etaples, and was so ill that on the 17th December a telegram was sent to his mother reporting that he was dangerously ill. Another telegram was sent to Hannah on the

27th December saying that there had been no improvement, and on the 5th January a third telegram was sent saying that his condition had improved. It must have been a very sad and difficult Christmas for the family, not knowing if Thomas would live or die. Thomas was well enough to be transferred back to the UK and he was sent to a hospital in Glasgow where he continued to improve until discharged on the 13th February 1917 and given 2 weeks' home leave. How happy everybody would have been to see their 'hero'.

Thomas had various home postings from the 14th February until the 2nd May 1917 when he again was sent to France. Unfortunately he was wounded with a gunshot wound to his left groin and he was hospitalised for 4 days at Ville d' Liege and then sent back to Eastbourne where he was treated from the 3rd August until the 4th September, before being given another 2 weeks' home leave.

In December 1917, Thomas was on the troopship H.T. 'ARAGON' heading for service in Egypt with the 12th Battalion of the L.N.L. Regiment. The ship arrived in Alexandria on the 30th December 1917, and it was permitted to enter the harbour, but later the authorities ordered it out again.

H.T. ARAGON *Image courtesy of Anne Yuill*

The 'ARAGON' was anchored outside the harbour without any protection and was torpedoed and sunk by the German submarine UC-34 in less than 15 minutes. 18 men of the Loyal North Lancashire Regiment lost their lives and drowned that night, including Private Thomas Robinson. His body was not recovered and he is remembered on the Chatby Memorial near Alexandria as well as on the Howden-le-Wear War Memorial.

1918

The final year of the war proved to be as deadly as the previous four years with more Howden-le-Wear men dying for their country. They were:

Denby Bennington, John Foster, Jacob Moses, James Coates, Thomas Eccles, Elias Williams, Herbert Fawell, Robert Clark and **Roderick Lauder.**

The Russian Revolution caused confusion and turmoil within Russia and their armed forces. Germany and Russia declared peace which allowed the German army to pull back all its forces from the Eastern Front to concentrate on the Western Front of the war. The massive increase in the Central Powers' manpower proved a very difficult time for the allied commanders.

The German Army made a final ferocious offensive starting in March 1918 on the Western Front in an attempt to force the allies to retreat. For three months they fought very hard but, by late summer, the allies managed to reverse the German advance and force them back towards their homeland.

It was a time of terrible loss on both sides and the Armistice was agreed on the 11th November 1918 after 1,559 days of war. The last allied casualty was killed on that day at 10.58am by a German sniper and was laid to rest near the grave of the first British casualty of the war, Private J. Parr, in St. Symphorien Military Cemetery in France.

Denby Bennington

Denby Bennington was born in July 1897 at Escomb near Bishop Auckland. He was the son of Jesse Bennington, a miner, and Susanna Bennington, and they lived at Hetton-le-Hole, near Sunderland. Denby's sister Adeline was born in 1900 and on the 1901 Census, Jesse, Suzanna and Adeline were still living in Hetton-le-Hole.

Denby was living at Escomb Post Office with his widowed grandmother Jane Denby, who was aged 65 and the head sub-postmistress in Escomb.

Also looking after Denby were his aunts, Emily Denby, a 26 year old infant school mistress, and Ada Florence Denby, aged 21, a home working knitting machinist.

Suzanna was pregnant and maybe this was a difficult pregnancy and Denby was sent to live with his grandmother and aunts to make life easier for the family. Sadly Suzanna and her new born baby daughter Suzanna both died in the late summer of 1901. Jane, Denby's grandmother, died in 1909 at the age of 74.

Sometime before 1911 Denby moved to live with his father's sister, Leah Tarn (later Dixon), and her family at Bridge Street, Howden-le-Wear. Leah, a widow, and two of her daughters were supported by her son Walter, a miner, the only wage earner in the family.

The 1911 Census shows that Denby's sister Adeline was by then living with a childless couple, John and Emily Hodgson, and their three lodgers, all of whom seem to have been involved in the catering trade in Archway Road, Highgate, in London.

Jesse Bennington, Denby's father, remarried in 1902 to Annie Jane Etherington, the daughter of John and Elizabeth Etherington of Bridge Street, Escomb and went on to have another five children, three of whom survived to adulthood. For a while they lived at 14 Valley Terrace in Howden-le-Wear, but later made their family home at Hamilton Row, Waterhouses. Jesse died in 1917. It appears that Denby and Adeline were not included in the new family of Jesse and probably had minimal contact with their father after he moved from Howden-le-Wear.

Denby was working as a grocer's assistant and still living with Leah in Valley Terrace, Howden-le-Wear, when he enlisted at Crook on the 12th January 1916 for the duration of the war. This was prior to conscription becoming compulsory. He was 18 years and 5 months old and 5 ft 6 ins tall. It is a well-known fact that many of those who enlisted were small and underweight. Denby named Adeline Bennington as his only living relative.

Initially Denby was assigned to the Army Reserve but was soon mobilised to the Welsh Regiment, regimental number 42067, and served with the 1st/5th Battalion. Denby spent some time at Gosforth Park training where he received ten days' confined to barracks for unofficially extending his leave.

Private Denby Bennington embarked at Southampton with the Egyptian Expeditionary Force on the 10th June 1917 and disembarked at Alexandria in Egypt on the 20th June. He joined his unit in the field on the 6th July and was hospitalised with diarrhoea on the 10th October, a complaint many soldiers in this theatre of war suffered from, no doubt as a result of the heat, flies and unsanitary conditions they endured. Denby rejoined his unit on the 18th January 1918.

It appears that Denby was killed or wounded in the Battle for Drages Hill in which the Welsh Regiment was involved. On the morning of the 13th March, the Hill was seized without opposition at 4.45am, but at daybreak the company sustained heavy fire from shells, machine guns and rifles. The company commander and 8 other ranks were killed and 75 other ranks were wounded. Denby, at the age of 21, was one of the soldiers killed in this battle. His body was not recovered, probably as a result of the heavy shelling of the area, and his name is inscribed on the Memorial at the Jerusalem War Cemetery. His few personal possessions were returned to Leah Dixon (formerly Tarn) and the death plaque and scroll were sent to his sister Adeline who was still living in Highgate, London. He was later awarded the Victory and British Medals.

John George Foster

John was born in 1888 in Witton-le-Wear to James and Elizabeth Foster. They lived at Victoria, Howden-le-Wear, and John had a brother Frederick, 10 years younger. In 1911, both John and his father were sanitary pipe makers.

Private John Foster enlisted with the Durham Light Infantry, number 3788, and then was transferred at some time to the 22nd (Service) Battalion of the Northumberland Fusiliers, number 35343, known as the Tyneside Scottish.   His DLI number indicates that he had been with the territorials prior to the outbreak of war. John most likely landed in France in January 1916 and he would have seen a great deal of front line action.

In March 1918, he was at Ervillers in northern France and he took part in the one of the bloodiest battles of the war. 21st March was the first day of the final offensive of the German army trying to retake lost ground and make a final push for Paris. During the previous week, John and his colleagues would have heard the enemy being reinforced and they would know a fierce battle would be following. The war diary for the Tyneside Scottish outlines very clearly the preparations being made ready for the attack. Lewis Gun classes and rifle instruction were held during the day, and by night the soldiers were reinforcing no-man's-land.

At 5am on the morning of the 21st, the intense enemy artillery barrage began, including gas shelling. The initial casualties were very heavy. By 11am the enemy had attacked in great numbers and outflanked the allied forward positions. By 1.30pm, the enemy had gained a sound footing and continued to advance. By 5pm, the enemy were on three sides of the 22nd Northumberland Fusiliers who, along with the 23rd and 25th, made a temporary HQ and all the military documents were burnt. A fighting retirement was then effected northwards.

By darkness, the losses were great and the village of Ervillers was completely destroyed. The lieutenant colonel had been killed, 11 officers were missing, and 6 officers were wounded. 30 other ranks were killed, 69 were wounded and 446 were declared missing, one of whom was John George Foster. Like so many, he is remembered on the Arras Memorial and also on the Howden-le-Wear War Memorial.

Jacob Moses

Jacob Moses appears to have a very tenuous connection with Howden-le-Wear, but his name is inscribed on the War Memorial. He was born in March 1881 to Robert and Isabella Moses in the village of Kirkley, Ravensworth, in Yorkshire, and Jacob was the sixth of eleven children.

The family was still at Ravensworth in 1891, and by 1901 Jacob, aged twenty one, was boarding with John and Mary Havis and their eight children at Toft Hill. His occupation was a coal miner/hewer. Five of this family, including Jacob, were working in the mines.

By 1911, Jacob was still single and was boarding in Commercial Street, Crook, with Charles and Susan Chambers and their three children and was still working as a coal miner.

Jacob enlisted in the army at Bishop Auckland during the first year of the war, and gave his residence as Howden-le-Wear, although there is no actual address recorded. This is his only apparent connection to Howden-le-Wear. Most likely he was boarding here and working in a local mine.

He went overseas on the 26th August 1915 and was soon promoted to corporal.   Jacob served with the 5th Battalion of the Alexandra, Princess of Wales' Own Yorkshire Regiment. His number was 17115 and he was serving in the Western European Theatre of war when he was killed in action on the 27th May 1918.

Jacob Moses' Medal Roll Card showing his regiment, number, date from which he served overseas, medal entitlement, and that he was killed.

Image courtesy of www.ancestry.co.uk

The 5th Yorkshire Regiment were on the right flank and the 4th East Yorkshires were on the left near Chevreux village. A German prisoner had informed their officers that there was to be a heavy attack with 2 to 3 hours' bombardment starting at 1am on the 27th May. Abnormal activity was also noted in the enemy trenches.

At 1am the bombardment started with shells, including gas. The brigade headquarters were struck and communication wires cut, causing great difficulties. The bombardment was the heaviest yet experienced by the soldiers and heavy casualties were inflicted, especially in the forward posts.

The enemy advanced and made good progress, engulfing the forward posts by 6.30am. The allied barrage continued for as long as possible, but many men were captured. Hand to hand fighting around the command posts was evident, but the battalion was overwhelmed. Heavy shelling continued and the survivors from the battalion withdrew toward the River Aisne. The brigadier general was captured and very few allied soldiers survived.

Corporal Moses was one of the soldiers who took part in this battle, but his body was not recovered. He is remembered on the Soissons Memorial in Aisne which commemorates over 4,000 officers and soldiers who died during this period. Jacob was later awarded the Victory and British Star Medals.

As well as being remembered on the Howden-le-Wear Memorial, Jacob is also remembered on the War Memorial at Ravensworth.

James Coates

James Coates was born on the 6th May 1884 in Witton-le-Wear and was known as Jimmy by the family. His birth was registered by his mother Mary Coates (née Colling) on 13th June 1884, who signed the register with her mark (X) as she could neither read nor write. His father, William Thomas Coates, was a coalminer. James was the youngest of 4 children, the others being Thomas, born 1871, Leonard, born 1879, and Jane Ann, born 1882. Jimmy's early working life was as a stonemason, but by 1906 he was mining coal.

Images courtesy of Billv Coates

He married Hannah Mills on the 31st July 1906 in the Wesleyan Methodist Chapel in Bishop Auckland. Hannah was 19 years old with no occupation and lived at Low Beechburn Farm. Her father was Robert Mills, also a coal miner. Jimmy was 22 when he married and was living at High Grange. Witnesses to the marriage were Jane Ann Coates, Jimmy's sister, and Margaret Watson Taylor. A miner called Francis Taylor used to lodge with the family when they lived in Swaledale and this could have been a relative. Hannah's grandparents came from the Isle of Skye and her grandfather had previously served with the Black Watch and spoke the Gaelic language.

Jimmy and Hannah lived in Howden-le-Wear after they married, but by 1911 had moved to Constantine Road, North Bitchburn. They had two daughters, Mary, born 1906, and Doris, born 1908, and two sons, William, born 1911, and Ralph, born 1913. Apparently all the children were born on the 24th day of the month. By the time Jimmy enlisted in the army in August 1915, the family was living at Valley Terrace, Howden-le-Wear, but at some time after this Hannah and her children moved back to 8 Low Row, North Bitchburn.

Before he went to war, Jimmy asked Leonard to look after Hannah and his children if anything should happen to him. This he did, and he always cared for them. Leonard was reported to have told Hannah many times that she had married the wrong brother. When Leonard died in the 1930s, he left a daughter who concealed the fact that Leonard had written a will which left everything to Jimmy's four children. When his daughter died in the 1990s, she did not leave a will and Leonard's original will was found. The families of Jimmy's children were contacted and all received a share of the will, 60 years after Leonard's death.

Jimmy volunteered to enlist in the East Yorkshire Regiment, number 19457, on the 27th August 1915. Why a Yorkshire regiment? This may have had something to do with the fact that his brothers and sister and both parents were born in Swaledale, Yorkshire, so there could have been strong Yorkshire allegiances.

Being a miner would have meant that he had skills required by the Royal Engineers in their tunnelling companies and, at some time, Jimmy transferred from the East Yorkshire Regiment to the 255th Tunnelling Company of the Royal Engineers, number197785. These men were sent down to dig tunnels under the German lines with the ultimate aim of blowing them up, which was an extremely dangerous and stressful task. In Geoff Dyer's book 'The Missing of the Somme' it tells how miners found themselves engaged in exactly the same activity they had pursued in peacetime, except that here their aim in burrowing beneath the earth was to lay hundreds of pounds of high explosives beneath the enemy's feet. The Germans, meanwhile, were engaged in similar operations and sometimes the two tunnel systems broke through to each other. Hundreds of feet beneath the earth, men clawed at one another's throats in these tunnels and beat one another to death with picks and shovels.

At the end of May 1918, the 255th Tunnelling Company were in Flanders, east of Abeele, but they were not underground, they were repairing trenches and wiring in an area called Boeschepe Lane. There were 20 officers, 1 medical officer and 350 other ranks working, but the war diary shows that there was a shortage of material and supplies which caused delays. During the night of the 30th/31st May, their camp was shelled and 35 other ranks were injured and killed.

One of these was Jimmy. On the 31st May, half of the section was deployed to dig the graves for their dead comrades. Jimmy was killed instantly and buried in the Lijssenthoek Military Cemetery, near Poperinge.

The grave of Jimmy Coates at Lijssenthoek Military Cemetery, near Poperinge.
Image courtesy of Billy Coates

Back home at Low Row, North Beechburn, Hannah would have received the dreaded telegram informing her of Jimmy's death. Mary was 11, Doris 9, William was 7 and Ralph was 5. James made a new will at the front and left everything to Hannah. After he died she received £11 11s 1d from the War Office in due pay, four months after his death.

Shortly after Jimmy's death, Hannah received the following letter from Sergeant Alec Marriott written on the 2nd June 1918:

> *Dear Mrs Coates,*
> *It is with the deepest sympathy that I write to you at this sad time that you are experiencing in the death of your dear husband. He was a good, trustworthy man whom everybody who knew him esteemed and respected. Under the painful circumstances, please accept all the consolations, his comrades and myself send you. I know you will be brave, also you know where to look for comfort and consolation, unto the one who gave his life for us. Whose words are; Greater love hath no man than this, that he lay down his life for his friends.*
>
> *We went to a service together the night he was called away. Jim always paid great attention to the things that matter most (the spiritual part). His good influence will live on, and he always tried to*

let his light shine before his fellow men. I cannot write and tell you any particulars except that he did not suffer, but was called suddenly away to his maker. It may be of some slight comfort to know he was buried quite decently, and the last rites performed by a Chaplain.

Sgt. G. Marriott 197791, No 1 Section, 255 Coy. R.E., B.E.F.

If there is anything that you think I could do please let me know. Give my love to Mary and the other children and my best wishes and prayers to yourself. May God bless you and help you to bear your burden.

Yours respectfully

A. G. Marriott

James is remembered on the War Memorial in Howden-le-Wear. Interestingly the Memorial states that his regiment was the East Yorkshire Regiment and not the Royal Engineers. As war memorials were provided by public subscription, the information to be written on the stone was also supplied by the family and there are anomalies across the memorials. Again the family allegiance to the East Yorkshire Regiment is evident.

There are no army records which survive for James Coates, but at the end of the war he was awarded three medals, the 1915 Star, the British Medal and the Victory Medal. Hannah would also have received the death plaque or 'dead man's penny' and a widow's pension for her and her children.

Hannah did not remarry but missed her 'Jimmy' all the rest of her life. Bill Coates, Hannah's grandson, could remember his grandmother talking to 'Jimmy' in the mid 1950s and there was a chair in the house known as 'Jimmy's chair'. Hannah later moved to Wheatbottom, Crook, and when she died, she was buried in Howden cemetery, near her father-in-law William Coates. Her son Ralph requested that his ashes also should be buried there.

Mary and Doris married two brothers called Pearson and returned to the family roots in Swaledale. One lived on a farm near Leyburn and the other farmed near Barnard Castle.

Thomas Eccles

Thomas Eccles is identified on the Howden-le-Wear War Memorial as having been in the Durham Light Infantry, and the initial research proved difficult. At first he appeared to have a Regimental number of 34887 for the DLI; 18769 for the Labour Sub Corps; and 47011 for the King's Own Scottish Borderers.

However, further research found that he was in fact a private in the East Yorkshire Regiment with a regimental number of 13330. His records also identify him as being in the 7th Service Battalion of the Army Service Corps (ASC). Given this information, he would have served with the East Yorkshires at the 2nd Battle of the Somme in August 1918. Therefore it was likely that, as he died on the 27th August 1918, he was killed during the Allied assault on Albert or Bapaume.

In 1891 the Eccles family are recorded as living in Stockton-on-Tees where William, Thomas's father, was employed as a 'puddler' in the iron and steel industry. Puddling was a process whereby molten iron was stirred by rods, which were consumed, and as such it was a method of making malleable wrought iron without charcoal. Their household in Hambleton Yard consisted of William and his wife Bridget and their three children, Mary, Ellen and James.

It is worth noting that, according to the 1881 Census, Thomas's grandfather, James Eccles, was born in County Tyrone, circa 1829. It is possible that, owing to the potato famine which ravaged Ireland in the 1840s, the Eccles family gave support to their relations and friends to escape the mass starvation that occurred in its aftermath by emigrating to England.

The 1901 census shows the family still living in Stockton-on-Tees with the five children. Thomas was aged 4 and his father and older brother James, aged 15, were recorded as steel workers.

The 1911 census identifies the Eccles family living at 32 Edith Street, Consett, in County Durham. His parents, William, now aged 50, and Bridget, also aged 50, had thirteen children. Thomas was 15 years old at this time and did not appear to be in employment. His father was a labourer in a smelting plant and his two older brothers, James, aged 25, and William, aged 20, were both employed as labourers at a blast furnace. There were a number of major iron and steel works in Consett, and these had attracted labour from all over the British Isles. Thomas's three younger sisters Tisina, aged 14, Annie, aged 12 and Margaret, aged 8, were in education, as was the youngest child in the family, Patrick, who was 6 years old.

However, there was a significant problem with the family research in that there is no record of where the Eccles family, including Thomas, lived in Howden-le-Wear. There is no doubt that the information given above is correct as it ties in with the military records concerning his enlistment, regimental number etc. These clearly show that Thomas Eccles, who was killed in action on 27th August 1918, was resident in Howden-le-Wear.

There was also some difficulty in identifying just which regiment Thomas Eccles originally enlisted into. There is evidence that he was serving with the Durham Light Infantry, number 34887, and this is how he is recorded on the Howden-le-Wear War Memorial. However, given the attrition rate, many divisions, battalions and brigades became undermanned and the remaining troops reconstituted into other divisions. This could possibly have seen Thomas being gradually moved from time to time, with the result that he finally ended up in the Army Service Corps as part of the East Yorks Regiment.

Thomas's military records identify him as being eligible for the 15 Star Medal with a qualifying date of September 9th 1915, being the date he arrived in France. He was just 19 years of age. This medal was awarded only to soldiers who had seen service in a theatre of war between 23rd November 1914 and 31st December 1915.

The 7th Service Battalion East Yorks landed in Boulogne on 14th July 1915 and Thomas arrived on the Western Front in the September. This was during a period where there was little change in terms of major battles and when both sides were consolidating their trenches. It was also a time when the Allied troops were losing 300 soldiers per day as a result of shelling and sniping by the enemy. Given that Thomas was on the Western Front in late 1915, he would have seen almost three years of active service before his death. He would have been engaged with the East Yorks as part of the 17th Northern Division in the Ypres campaign in 1915, the First Battle of the Somme in 1916, Passchendaele in 1917, and the Second Battle of the Somme in 1918.

The regimental badges of the East Yorkshire Regiment and the Army Service Corps, in which Thomas Eccles served.

As a member of the Army Service Corps attached to the 7th Service Battalion East Yorkshire Regiment, Thomas would have been part of a vast army of soldiers supporting the front line troops by providing them with the essentials of war. The Army Service Corps have been described as 'the unsung heroes of the Great War'. They provided food, equipment, ammunition, clothes and all that was required by the front line soldiers.

The Army Service Corps Bakery.   *Image courtesy of www.1914-1918.net*

They dug trenches, moved guns along the front line, transported troops backwards and forwards and supplied the daily provisions needed to ensure the front lines were maintained. By 1918, the Army Service Corps had some 10,547 officers, and 315,334 men. They supported over 3 million troops and 500,000 horses with 90 million units of bread, 67 million units of beef, 250,000 units of forage and 13 million gallons of petrol.

The provisions usually started in Britain and were shipped from the Channel ports such as Le Havre and Calais. There they were allocated to various depots to be distributed along the 400 mile Western Front. The French railway system was used to transport the goods from the ports to a point as near to the front line as they could. Regulating Stations nearer the front would further divide the goods to meet the specific needs of their battle area. From this point the goods were transported by either horses or motor vehicles up to the Infantry Base Depots nearer to the trenches. In some areas the Royal Engineers laid support rail tracks directly to the reserve trenches.

By 1916, the Army Service Corps was embedded into the various regiments and this saw them having to work much nearer to the front than previously.

A column of the Army Service Corps travelling through a French village.

Image courtesy of www.1914-1918 .net

The main communication arteries were targeted by the Germans and it saw them under frequent bombardment. As a result, the supplies to the front line were mainly carried forward at night, in the hope of escaping the shelling under the cover of darkness. However, if ammunition was urgently needed, then it had to be delivered no matter what the risks involved.

On the 21st March 1918, the Germans launched 'Operation Michael'. The German Army had been reinforced by troops from the Eastern Front after their Armistice with Russia. Thousands of infantry men from the 17th, 2nd and 18th German Armies attacked from their front line after a five hour artillery bombardment. Some 3.2 million shells were destined to land on the Allied front line during the first day. To the German infantry's advantage there was fog, and many of their assault troops reached the Allied lines without being spotted.

The southern part of the British Fifth Army was broken and the Germans advanced for three days. However, they gradually outstripped their supply lines and the troops began to tire, without the essentials such as water, food, and ammunition, the very types of supplies Thomas Eccles was helping to provide to the East Yorkshire Regiment. As a result, the German advance on the Somme gradually came to a halt.

Nevertheless, they had gained some 1,000 square miles of territory, including Albert and Bapaume where so many Allied lives had been lost during the fighting in 1916. The shortages of reserves, ammunition and horses made it impossible for the Germans to launch further attacks in this area and on 5th April 1918 General Ludendorff sent a message to say the Michael Offensive was 'terminated'. The German offensive had cost 31,000 killed, 20,000 missing and 190,000 wounded. At the same time the Allies had suffered over 160,000 killed or wounded and 90,000 men were taken prisoner.

Throughout the war, many British brigades and battalions were merged and reconstituted because of the high number of casualties. The 7th Service Battalion, formed in Beverley, Yorkshire, in 1914, was part of the New Army. Subsequently, the East Yorks came under orders of the 50th Brigade in the 17th Northern Division. These were part of the British Third Army led by General Byng.

Military records confirm Private Thomas Eccles as being part of the East Yorks Army Service Corps in 1918 and, as such, involved in the Second Battle of the Somme.

By the summer of 1918, the Allies had regrouped and were on the offensive in the Somme area. This included the Battle of Amiens, which began on the 8th August, and the Allies rapidly progressed eastwards for a number of miles. The advance saw the Allies recapture much of the ground lost during 'Operation Michael'. These battles marked the end of trench warfare owing to the combined use of air power and tanks supporting the infantry troops. These battles in August became known as the 'Hundred Days' Offensive' and the 8th August 1918 was seen as a 'devastating day' for the German Army.

On 21st August, the British Third Army and USA 11 Corps launched an attack on Albert and pushed the Germans back to the Hindenburg Line.

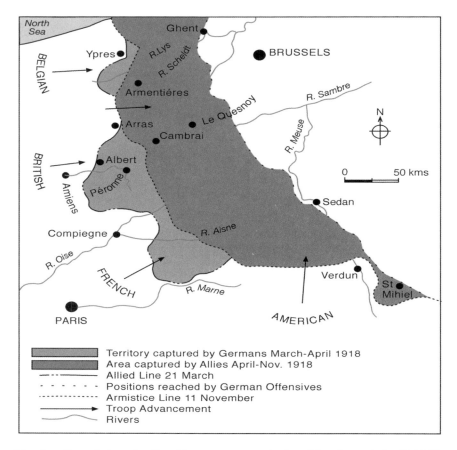

The territory taken by the German army during March and April 1918, and the change by the Armistice, just six months later.

Image courtesy of www.1914-1918.net

The same regiments were involved in the Second Battle of Bapaume, from the 21st August to the 3rd September and Bapaume was captured on the 29th August. As identified above, the East Yorks were part of this assault and, given that Thomas died on the 27th August 1918, it is most likely he became a casualty during this fierce infantry fighting.

Private Thomas Eccles was buried in Fler Cemetery some 3 miles south west of Bapaume, and 10 miles north east of Albert. The Fler Commonwealth War Cemetery held 3,473 graves, 2,263 of which were of unidentified servicemen, 'known only to God'. Included in these numbers were 16 East Yorkshire Regimental graves, and Thomas was recorded as being buried in Grave 11 K5.

Fler Cemetery, Picardy, France, where Private Thomas Eccles was laid to rest in August 1918. His grave is on the right hand side of the central path.
Image courtesy of www.cwgc.org

As Thomas entered the army during the first year of the war, he saw lengthy military service. Unfortunately, the military records are not available to identify in detail his previous postings, or the front line action he saw. Nevertheless, it is likely that Thomas was killed during one of the most significant battles of the war. The Battles of Albert and Bapaume were identified as forcing the end of German resistance on the Western Front in the Somme salient.

WWI posters used to encourage Irish volunteers to join the British Army.
Image courtesy of www.1914-1918.net

Given that the Eccles family originated in Ireland, it was for Thomas not 'a long way to Tipperary' but 'a long way to Tyrone'. Thomas was descended from Irish stock and he, along with thousands of troops marshalled from around the British Empire, played his part in determining a victorious outcome for the Allied forces.

Elias Williams: A Welsh Connection 'From Rotten Row to Shiney Row'

On 15th September 1866, Elias Ellis Williams was born in Soughton Mountain, Northrop, Flintshire, Wales, to Edwin Williams and his wife Hannah Ellis. He grew up living in Mold, Flintshire, until the family decided to leave Wales in search of work.

They found that employment was available in the many new coal mines and coke works being opened in South West Durham and by 1881 had moved to 13 White Lea Square, Billy Row, Crook, with their two sons, John and Elias.

Continuing their search for work in the coal mines, the family moved to 83 Liddell Street, Cornsay Colliery, where, in 1891, Edwin, now 61 years old, and both his sons, John and Ellis, worked in the local pit. In 1892, they moved to Thistleflat, Crook.

Two years later, on 30th December 1893, Ellis married Elizabeth Race from Woodifield Row, Crook, and moved back to Helmington Row where, on 1st November 1894, their son Elias was born and registered there on 3rd December 1894. Unfortunately it appears that Elizabeth did not survive very long after giving birth to another son, Thomas Edwin Williams, and died from typhoid fever and bowel perforation, aged 28 years, on 27th October 1899 whilst living at 19 High Row, Roddymoor. It is interesting to note that neither Ellis nor Elizabeth could sign his or her name, as the relevant registration certificates were signed only with a certified 'X'.

Elias Ellis, Elias junior and Thomas Edwin then moved in with John Williams and domestic housekeeper, Bessie Coulson, a 59 year old widow, at 32 Lumley Yard, Bridge Street, Crook. This was a low location situated close to the heavily polluted, stinking Beechburn Beck. Nearby houses were called 'Rotten Row' as it was such an unhealthy place to live. Disease and fever were commonplace as poor housing and lack of proper sanitation took their toll on people living there. These sub-standard dwellings have long since been demolished but, in 1901, Elias Ellis and his two sons survived living there, no doubt wishing for better times.

On 23rd May 1908 Ellis, now aged 41 years, married Charlotte Anne Williams at Bishop Auckland Register Office. Elias junior was then 13 years old and the family moved to Arthur Street in Crook, a far better location, and conditions appear to have improved. Ellis and Charlotte had two more children, Edith Annie and Edward, and by 1911 Elias junior, then 16 years old, was also working with his father in the mines as a 'helper-up'.

The family's next move was to Howden-le-Wear where they settled in a house in Valley Terrace. These pleasant houses had an open aspect with gardens and were locally known as 'Shiney Row', possibly because of the bright sunlight that was reflected from the windows every sunny afternoon and evening.

Private Elias Williams.
Image courtesy of Howden-le-Wear History Society

When the First World War broke out in 1914, Elias was only 19 years old. He enlisted at Spennymoor into the King's Royal Rifle Corps and Private Rifleman R/17219 later transferred to the Rifle Brigade (Prince Consort's Own) 1st/8th London Regiment, Number B/203034.

The King's Royal Rifle Corps' sixteen battalions were continuously in action from 1914, when the first shots were fired at Mons, until November 1918. Most of the fighting was on the Western Front.

At Ypres, such was the speed and power of the rifle fire that the Germans were famously deceived into thinking they were up against entrenched machine guns. In the same battle, three companies of the corps' 1st Battalion were surrounded and annihilated. At the battle of Cambrai, in November 1917, the corps' 10th and 11th Companies were attacked on three sides and destroyed. The corps lost three more battalions, the 7th, 8th and 9th, on the first day of the German Spring offensive on March 21st 1918. The King's Royal Rifle Corps lost a total of 13,000 officers and men in the 4 year conflict.

On 14th October 1918, less than a month before the Armistice ceasefire, Elias Williams, aged 23 years, was reported killed in action in Flanders Fields in France. His body was never recovered.

His step-mother Charlotte and father Elias were informed of their son's death and in due course received his medals. They passed the rest of their days living in 'Shiney Row', but 30 Valley Terrace would never again shine so brightly following their sad loss. Elias Ellis passed away, aged 66 years, on 10th September 1933.

Elias Williams' medal and death plaque along with the letter sent from the King to all bereaved next of kin.
Image courtesy of Howden-le-Wear History Society

Elias junior is commemorated in the Lievin Communal Cemetery Extension in France and also on the Howden-le-Wear War Memorial.

Herbert Britton Fawell

Herbert Fawell appears first on Census records in 1891 as a child aged three months. His father's family had moved to Crook prior to 1851 after leaving Hauxwell in Yorkshire, and Herbert was one of Matthew's children from his second marriage to Margaret Kidd. They lived at West Road, Crook, where they remained for well over 30 years. Life revolved round the colliery and brickworks, with Matthew working above ground as a mason, whilst his sons were labourers.

In 1912 Herbert married Mary Dunn and on the 22nd June 1915, aged 24 years and 6 months, Herbert joined the army and registered for four years' service or the duration of the war with the 8th Durham Light Infantry.

It seemed that Herbert and Mary may have separated as, in his army records, there is a statement signed on 29th January 1915 and witnessed by a magistrate, stating that Herbert would pay Mary Jane Nicholson of Valley Terrace, Howden-le-Wear, 2s 6d a week for an illegitimate child born on the 26th December 1914. This would be paid from the 30th January 1915 until the child was 14 years of age or died. On the 4th February 1916, he also signed over 4 pence a week from his army pay for the child before he was sent overseas with the British Expeditionary Force in France.

Herbert had recorded his marriage date as the 23rd November 1912 and the record shows that Mary was living at Howden Square, Howden-le-Wear. Mary Jane was living at Valley Terrace, Howden-le-Wear, and was noted as the person to whom he was making a compulsory payment. When Herbert enlisted in the army his address was Holly Terrace, Howden-le-Wear, so it appears that he was not living with either his wife or his child's mother.

At a later unconfirmed date, Herbert received a gunshot wound to his ear and it is not clear when, where or how this happened or whether this was the cause of his death.

However, Private 301021 Fawell, who died on October 17th 1918, is commemorated at the Cologne Memorial, on the southern side of the city. A clue to his death is given in historical information from the Commonwealth War Graves Commission, which reveals that the small Memorial:

> *"... commemorates 25 servicemen of the United Kingdom who died in Germany and who have no known grave. Of these, 19 are known to have died as prisoners and their places of burial are not recorded. The other six died after the Armistice by drowning and their bodies were not recovered."*

Herbert's name is on the bottom plinth of the Howden-le-Wear War Memorial and was added after the initial names were inscribed.

Mary later married Reginald Griffiths in the spring of 1919.

Robert Taylor Clark

When George Clark married Amelia Davison in 1898, he named his first born son after his brother Robert Taylor Clark. This young man travelled to Bishop Auckland after his father's death and volunteered to enlist in the 7th Battalion of the East Yorkshire Regiment, number 54729. Who knows why? Possibly to avenge his father's death, for money to support the family now that his father was no longer providing, or perhaps just following in his footsteps.

The 7th (Service) Battalion was mobilised for war on 14th July 1915 and landed at Boulogne and engaged in various actions on the Western Front including, in 1916, the Battles of Albert and Delville Wood; in 1917, the First and Second battles of The Scarpe, the Capture of Roeux and the First

Private R. T. Clark.
Image courtesy of William Clark

and Second Battles of Passchendaele, and in 1918, the Battles of St Quentin, Bapaume, Amiens, Albert, Bapaume, Haverincourt, the Pursuit to the Selle and the Battle of the Sambre.

Private Robert Taylor Clark, aged 20 years, was killed at the Battle of the Sambre, one of the final battles of the war, on 27th October 1918, only two weeks before the ceasefire and Armistice.

Following Robert's death, Remembrance Cards were distributed and there were memorials to Robert recorded in France and at home. He was

119

The grave of Robert Clark at Romeries Communal Cemetery Extension.
Image courtesy of William Clark

buried in Romeries Communal Cemetery Extension and was also commemorated on the Howden-le-Wear War Memorial.

After his father George had been killed in action in 1915, Amelia was left to cope with bringing up the family. She subsequently registered George Junior into the Mixed School on the 21st August 1917, and Edgar into Infants on the 22nd July 1917 and on to the Mixed School on the 13th April, 1920. Colin was the last child to be registered at Howden school by Amelia on the 3rd April 1922.

What an enormous task for the woman to achieve single handed, as well as coping with the death of her oldest son Robert. The oldest son, William, was working, but she still had six children to look after and bring up, perhaps with some help from her daughters, Irene and Edna.

Amelia Clark, widowed, eventually moved from Victoria Row, where the houses were condemned and demolished, to 8 Church Street, Howden-le-Wear, where she lived with two sons until her death from heart failure in September 1952, aged 77 years. Her death was registered at Crook by one son Lenneth, and a certificate issued to her younger son George who was then living at Witton Park. George was the father of William Clark, grandson of Sapper George Clark, and nephew of Private Robert Taylor Clark.

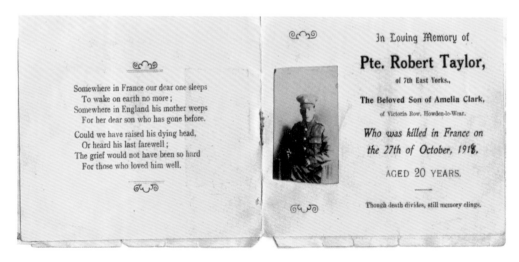

In Loving Memory of

Pte. Robert Taylor,

of 7th East Yorks.,

The Beloved Son of Amelia Clark,

of Victoria Row, Howden-le-Wear.

Who was killed in France on the 27th of October, 1918.

AGED 20 YEARS.

Though death divides, still memory clings.

Somewhere in France our dear one sleeps
To wake on earth no more ;
Somewhere in England his mother weeps
For her dear son who has gone before.

Could we have raised his dying head,
Or heard his last farewell ;
The grief would not have been so hard
For those who loved him well.

The Memorial Card for Robert Taylor Clark that would have been shared by many people within Howden-le-Wear.

Image courtesy of William Clark

Roderick Lauder

Roderick Lauder was born in 1898 and was the ninth child and younger brother of Elijah Roderick who also made the ultimate sacrifice during the Great War. The family story is told in the section on Elijah who died in 1916.

There is little information about Roderick's war service, not even the year he enlisted. Recorded are his rank and regimental number, Private 83642, and the fact that he served with the 12th/13th Battalion of the Northumberland Fusiliers.

His family, having lost Elijah in 1916, and with the war nearing its end, must have been hoping for Roderick's safe return, but their younger son's battalion had been involved in the final advance of the allies in Picardy and casualties occurred. Along with others of his group, Private Roderick Lauder was killed in action on November 4th 1918, just seven days before the cessation of hostilities.

Roderick was buried in a small French cemetery near Fontaine-au-Bois with over 90 other men who died in October and November of that year.

LAUDER, R	
Rank:	Private
Service No:	83642
Date of Death:	04/11/1918
Regiment/Service:	Northumberland Fusiliers
	12th/13th Bn.
Grave Reference	C. 1.
Cemetery	FONTAINE-AU-BOIS COMMUNAL CEMETERY

Private Roderick Lauder's memorial on the CWGC records.

Image courtesy of www.cwgc.org

❖ *DIED AT HOME*

William Wilson

The Census recorded in 1911 shows that William Wilson lived at the Surtees Hotel with his 42 year old widowed mother Dinah, his father William having died in 1908. Also there were his siblings, Elizabeth, Sarah and Robert. William was an above ground labourer in the colliery. All of the family had been born in Middlestone Moor, near Spennymoor.

The Surtees Hotel run by Dinah Wilson, the mother of William Wilson. The notice board above the door showed the landlord as William Wilson who died in 1908, so the photo predates that. It was highly possible that one of the children in the picture is William Wilson who served in France and who died of influenza at the age of 25 years.

Image courtesy of Howden-le-Wear History Society

123

HOWDEN-LE-WEAR INSTITUTE A.F.C.

William was a keen footballer and in 1910 - 11 he played for the Howden-le-Wear Institute Amateur Football club and they won the 1st Division League. William is on the front row, second from the right.

Image courtesy of Howden-le-Wear History Society

On his enlistment in September 1914 at Bishop Auckland, William was described as being 5 ft 7 ins tall, weighing 156 lbs, having brown hair and eyes and a clear complexion. He was a Primitive Methodist and on enlistment was 22 years and 4 months old. William was given the number 18862 and was assigned to the Northumberland Fusiliers. He was one of the thousands of men who was caught up in the excitement of war and believed that it would be over by Christmas. He went to training camp and then was posted overseas to France.

A year later, whilst engaging with the enemy between Vermilles and Loos, William received an incapacitating gunshot wound to his left hand and was also subject to gas poisoning. Medical Board reports recognised that the damage to his hand was permanent and he was given a final discharge with a pension on the grounds that he was no longer fit for war service. This was registered on the 4th April 1918, with effect from 31st October 1916. Private Wilson's military character was 'very good' and he was a 'well-behaved man'.

William was awarded a Silver War Badge which was issued to servicemen who had been honourably discharged owing to wounds or sickness. It was intended to be worn on civilian clothes on the right breast. It is known that that some people, especially women, gave white feathers to what appeared able bodied men as a sign of disgust that they were not in uniform. The silver badge ensured that wounded servicemen were treated with respect and not hostility. He also received the 1914 - 15 Star, British War Medal and Victory Medal after 2 years and 55 days of service.

William returned to Valley Terrace in Howden-le-Wear and to work at North Bitchburn Colliery where he was given a job that he could do despite his injury. In 1916, he married Margaret Ann Carr. William and Margaret saw the Armistice together, but shortly afterwards he contracted influenza and died of pneumonia on the 6th December 1918 at the age of 25.

He was buried in St Mary's churchyard, Howden-le-Wear.

The grave of William and Dinah Wilson, with son William also remembered, in Howden-le-Wear cemetery.

Image courtesy of Howden-le-Wear History Society

FE 394952

CERTIFIED COPY of an ENTRY
Pursuant to the Births and Deaths Registration Act 1953

Registration District Auckland

Death in the Sub-district of Hamsterley   in the County of Durham

1918.

No.	When and where died	Name and surname	Sex	Age	Occupation	Cause of death	Signature, description and residence of informant	When registered	Signature of registrar
Columns:-	1	2	3	4	5	6	7	8	9
271	Sixth December 1918 1 Valley Terrace Witton le Wear RD	William Wilson	Male	26 years	Coalminer (Hewer)	(1) Influenza 3 days (2) Pneumonia 3 days No PM Certified by W H MacGranhan MB	Thos Smith Brother in Law Present at the death Surtees Hotel Howden-le-Wear	Seventh December 1918	J E Townend Registrar

Certified to be a true copy of an entry in a register in my custody.

D. A. Morris   _Deputy_   Superintendent Registrar

08-08-2014   Date

CAUTION: THERE ARE OFFENCES RELATING TO FALSIFYING OR ALTERING A CERTIFICATE AND USING OR POSSESSING A FALSE CERTIFICATE. ©CROWN COPYRIGHT

WARNING: A CERTIFICATE IS NOT EVIDENCE OF IDENTITY.

126

Percy Cooke

Although he was to serve in the Durham Light Infantry, Percy Cooke was a native of Yorkshire. He was born in Liversedge in West Yorkshire on the 5th January 1896. The record of his birth shows his surname spelt without the final 'e', and this discrepancy occurs elsewhere.

Percy Cooke with his parents and sister Elsie.

Images courtesy of Joyce Charlton

The Census of 1901, again recording the surname without the final 'e', shows the family living at the Gas House in Boston Spa, Yorkshire. His father, Thomas Albert, aged 29, also born in Liversedge, was a gas engineer and gas works manager connected with a colliery, gas being a bye-product of coal production. His mother, Sarah, aged 30, was born in Mirfield in Yorkshire. Percy was the oldest child, aged 5, and he had two sisters at that time, Elsie, aged 2, who died young, and Mabel, aged 6 months.

The 1911 Census records the surname with a final 'e', and shows the family living at Batts, West Auckland, in County Durham. Thomas Albert moved with his job, and was working at Randolph Coke Ovens at Evenwood. Percy was also a colliery worker, and is shown in the Census as being a bank hand. The family had now increased with the birth of Percy's two further sisters, Ada, aged 3, and Mary Ellen (Nellie), aged 9 months. A further sister, Margaret, was born in 1914.

The family later moved to Valley Terrace in Howden-le-Wear, Thomas Albert now holding a senior position at the bye-product section of Bowden Close Colliery at Helmington Row, where Percy also worked. The colliery was owned by Messrs Pease & Partners, and *Whellan's 1894 Directory of County Durham* states that all the output was converted into coke, there being 135 ovens. We are told that Helmington Row was then little more than a straggling row of cottages, inhabited by the miners employed at Bowden Close Colliery. Bowden Close itself was entirely a colliery village. The Miners' Institute consisted of billiard room, reading room and library, which received books from the Yorkshire Union. In 1914, the colliery employed 1,544 men.

In June 1914, shortly before the outbreak of war, a severe blow struck Percy's family when his mother died as a result of the birth of his youngest sister, Margaret, on the 23rd June. Not only did Percy have to come to terms with the death of his mother, but within a matter of weeks, the family was split up as his youngest sisters were sent away to live with other family members. Mabel, the oldest, now 14, had to take on the responsibility of staying at home to look after her father and Percy, while Ada, now 6, Nellie, aged 3, and the newborn Margaret all went away to live with uncles and aunts in Yorkshire.

We also know that there was a creative side to Percy's nature. The report of the Annual Meeting of the Witton-le-Wear Institute, held on the 11th February 1915, recorded that 'The sale of the inspiring poem "A Call to Arms" composed by Mr Percy Cooke has released 16s and 8d and this amount has been handed over to Mrs Lishman's fund for the purchase of wool and other materials for the making of socks and garments for our soldiers and sailors abroad. Mr Cooke is planning to enlist in the Army later this year as soon as he is 19 years of age. He currently lives at Valley Terrace, Howden-le-Wear.'

There is some confusion in dates in this report as Percy was already 19 years of age at the time of this meeting, his birthday being in January, but he did indeed enlist in the 6th DLI on the 14th August 1915, with the regimental number 6/4224.

The 6th DLI, formed in August 1914, was originally stationed at Bishop Auckland as part of the 50th (Northumbrian) Division, a formation of the Territorial Force, but, after moving to various different bases, it was mobilised in April 1915 and landed at Boulogne. By the 23rd April, the division had concentrated in the area of Steenvoorde. It had arrived just as the German army had attacked nearby Ypres, using poison gas for the first time, and the division was rushed into the battle. A month later the formation became the 151st Brigade of the 50th (Northumbrian) Division, and was engaged in various actions on the Western Front.

Although he started in the 6th DLI, Percy transferred to the 9th DLI with the regimental number 5/7176. The 9th DLI was formed at exactly the same time as the 6th, but it was originally stationed at Gateshead. Both battalions were then moved to Ravensworth Park, from which time they had identical records as part of the 50th Division.

The division remained in France and Flanders, and in 1915 took part in various phases of the Second Battle of Ypres. The following year, the division took part in various phases of the Battle of the Somme. The Somme offensive, which started at dawn on the 1st July 1916, had by the end of October been waged in several phases for four months without any decisive result, and with many thousands of casualties on both sides.

In the final days of October 1916, although the weather was warmer, heavy rain and gale force winds, particularly at night, were soaking the ground over which the next attack would be made and making the mud deeper and thicker. By this time, conditions in and behind the battle front were so bad that the infantry, sometimes soaked to the skin and almost exhausted even before they launched an attack, were often forced to struggle painfully forward through the mud under heavy fire against their objectives.

The offensive continued on both sides of the River Ancre. On the 30th October 1916, a limited attack was planned aimed at eliminating the German salients north east of Eaucourt L'Abbaye and north of Gueudecourt. The former salient enclosed the Butte of Warlencourt, a barrow or tumulus about 40 ft high, which gave an important vantage point to whoever held it. The attack took place on the 5th November 1916, after a wet night followed by gales, that were still blowing strong when the brigade, which had spent the night in trenches filled with cold mud up to the thighs, with great difficulty clambered out to its last battle on the Somme.

The 1st/9th Battalion of the DLI commanded by Lieutenant Colonel Bradford, of 'Fighting Bradford' and 'Witton Park' fame, was tasked with capturing the Butte and the quarry just west of it. Whilst the Butte provided the enemy with good observation of the ground towards High Wood and Martinpuich, it was not, at this time, considered to be of any great military value. It did, however, lie in the path of the advance and, it seems, no one had given consideration to going round it and isolating it, leaving the enemy forces dug into the Butte to be mopped up later.

While the Germans sustained heavy losses, the British losses were also very high, with the 9th Durhams losing 17 officers killed, wounded or missing,

30 non-commissioned officers and men killed, and 250 wounded and 140 missing.

While the 6th and 8th Brigades were beset by problems, particularly as a result of the terrible conditions presented by the mud, the 9th "B" Company, of which Percy was a member, initially had some success and passed over two lines of German trenches. However, the 9th was now lacking in support as a result of the problems which affected the other battalions. But at about 3.30pm, the enemy, having already made several unsuccessful counter-attacks, attacked again, and the 9th Battalion were forced back. Watchers from the other Durham trenches saw the solitary figure of a 9th Battalion man pause for a moment at the summit of the Butte and then pass down the other side into a desperate mêlée that continued all afternoon and far into the night.

At 5.00 p.m. Lieutenant Colonel Bradford reported to brigade:

> *"We have been driven out of Gird Front Line. I believe my Posts there have been captured. I have tried to get back, but the enemy is in considerable force and is still counter attacking."*

Desperate hand to hand fighting took place during the afternoon. The officers and men of the 9th Battalion were now extremely weary and had suffered heavy losses. After four hours of sustained and heavy bombardment from the enemy artillery, a final counter attack was launched against the battalion positions.

Lieutenant Colonel Bradford's final report includes the following:

> *"At about 11 pm, Battalions of the Prussians delivered a fresh counter attack. They came in great force from our front and also worked round from both flanks. Our men were overwhelmed. Many died fighting. Others were compelled to surrender. It was only a handful of men who found their way back to Maxwell Trench and they were completely exhausted by their great efforts and the strain of the fighting.*
>
> *We have been driven out of Butte Alley by a strong attack and 9th DLI and 6th DLI are now in Maxwell trench . . . and we cannot get back to Butte Alley. All our Posts are captured or driven back."*

For the 9th DLI, although this was a disappointing close to the offensive in which so much had been accomplished, there was no dishonour in having failed against such opponents.

For Percy Cooke, this desperate battle marked the end of his active role in the war. He was one of those captured, having been taken prisoner at Le Serre, and was to spend the rest of the war in various Prisoner of War camps.

The first Prisoner of War record, officially stamped 29th November 1916, shows that Percy was taken to the town of Cambrai, only a short distance inside the German occupied territory. A superimposed stamp showed that his family had been informed of his capture. The German army occupied Cambrai on the 25th August 1914, and, despite numerous attempts by the allied forces to regain the town, they remained there until the 9th October 1918 when Canadian forces liberated the town. Cambrai was used as a major command and logistics centre, and the Germans also set up a number of hospitals there. It was in one of these hospitals that Percy was to spend various periods of his time as a prisoner of war.

Further records, of which there are eight in all, the last being stamped 12th February 1918, show that he also spent time at the prison camp at Dülmen, the military hospital at Minden, and finally at Friedrichsfeld prison. Several times he returned to spend time at the military hospital at Cambrai.

Several of the records show that he was unwounded, so his periods in hospital could not have been as a result of any injury. However, we know from the evidence of his late sister, passed on to her family, that he eventually returned home after the war suffering from tuberculosis. As his Prisoner of War records state that he was unwounded following his capture, is it reasonable to assume that his periods in hospital were as a result of the start of his illness, and the deterioration in his medical condition?

Following his repatriation, Percy was eventually discharged from the army on the 29th May 1919. He was awarded the Victory Medal and the British War Medal. After his return, in honour of his war service, he was also awarded a medal by his former colleagues at the colliery.

The front of the medal with shield and initials 'PC'. The back of the medal is inscribed:
'Bowden Close Bye Product Plant presented to Private. P. Cooke, D.L.I. by fellow workmen for Army Service during War 1914 - 1918'
Image courtesy of Joyce Charlton

Percy was engaged to Ethel (Ettie) Raine of Valley Terrace, Howden-le-Wear. He never married owing to his illness which led to his early death. In the summer months he would spend a lot of time in a shed at the top of the garden in order to breathe the fresh air. Ethel helped to nurse him. She never married, and continued to live at home with two of her brothers.

Percy was living at 22 Valley Terrace, Howden-le-Wear, at the time of his death. He died on the 1st September, 1923. His death certificate shows the cause of his death as "Phthisis Pulmonalis" (tuberculosis). His funeral was held on the 5th September 1923, and was conducted by the vicar of St Mary's Church, the Reverend Bertram Stone Spencer. He was buried in the churchyard of St Mary the Virgin at Howden-le-Wear.

The National Probate Calendar (Index of Wills and Administrations) holds the following record:

> 'COOKE Percy of 22 Valley-terrace, Howden-le Wear, County Durham died 1 September 1923. Administration Durham 5 December to Thomas Albert Cooke bye product worker. Effects £150 5s 4d.'

Although he survived the war, Percy Cooke was nevertheless a casualty of the war as a result of the illness which he developed while serving in the army, and which led to his early death at the age of only 27.

❖ *FROM FIR TREE TO*
FRANCE AND FLANDERS

The men who went to fight from Fir Tree

—

1914 - 1918

—

**farm hand, forestry worker, saw miller,
miner, publican and boy scout, railwayman,
cart drivers and the gentry
to become
soldiers of the
British Expeditionary Force**

All of the men from Fir Tree who served during the Great War lived or worked in and around the village of Fir Tree at the start of or during the Great War. At the time Fir Tree was described as a small village situated on a bend on the West Auckland to Corbridge Road, now known as the A68.

On the 4th August 1914, Britain declared war on Germany after it invaded Belgium. At this time Britain's Army was comparatively small compared to those of its European neighbours of France and Germany. The British Army was more like a police force to protect her commonwealth, comprising only six divisions. Fir Tree had been expanding over the previous few years as mining developed all around the village, primarily through Harperley Collieries. The principal owners of Harperley Collieries Company Ltd were Thomas Finley J.P. of Allotment House, Fir Tree, and John Thomas Hird of Thistleflat Farm near Crook.

Fir Tree Drift Mine, 1913.   Many of these men would soon be volunteering to serve their country in foreign fields.

Image courtesy of Howden-le-Wear History Society

The Duke of York Public House c1900.

Image courtesy of Howden-le-Wear History Society

Families were moving into the village with four new terraces being built during 1911, all with allotment gardens to grow their own vegetables or keep a few chickens. One or two families also kept a pig or two. The gardens for Harperley Terrace were situated adjacent to Coronation Terrace.

Institute Terrace, Fir Tree, c1900. The Vitty family lived in the middle of this terrace.

Image courtesy of Howden-le-Wear History Society

Effectively the village hall had been rebuilt and there were two public houses, three shops, a new school and two churches. **This photograph is of the school children in 1900.**

Image courtesy of Howden-le-Wear History Society

Blacksmith's shop in Fir Tree on the right looking towards Harperley.

The second photograph shows the blacksmith at work.

Images courtesy of Howden-le-Wear History Society

When we look back at this period in village life, everyone thinks how quiet, pleasant and quaint it was, but then think about what it was really like. The working week was on average a 10-12 hour day, six days a week, and after a hard day's work toiling on the farm or down the mine a worker could enjoy a nice hot bath. Yes! – a 'tin' bath in front of the fire to fill and empty by hand. The toilets were earth closets at the bottom of the yard and most of the houses were two up two down with a coal fire in one room to keep you warm, heat your water, and cook your food. In some cases there were three generations living in one house. There was no electricity in the village, as it arrived in Fir Tree only in 1939.

With most of the families working five and a half or six days a week, it left little time for a social life. For those over 21 there were two public houses, and the landlord of The Fir Tree Inn was a Jack Goodwin.

The Fir Tree Inn on the right on the road leading towards Howden-le Wear.
Image courtesy of Howden-le-Wear History Society

The newly erected Institute, known as the Fir Tree Jubilee and Coronation 1911 Institute, was on the site of the old village hall. The land had been provided by Frances Dorothea Stobart and George Herbert Stobart, her son. It was built by Thomas Finley of Allotment House and John Thomas Hird of Thistleflat Farm, Crook. As the men under the age of 21 were not allowed in the public houses, the Institute gave them somewhere to go, with a full size snooker table and piano.

Twice a week William Vitty changed hats from miner to scoutmaster, at first using the hall for their meetings. Frances Dorothea Stobart and George Herbert Stobart provided the scouts with a piece of land at the bottom of The Well Green on which to erect a scout hut which was to the south of where the War Memorial now stands.

Postcard of servicemen sent from scout James McAdam to the scoutmaster, William Vitty. *Image courtesy of John Alderson.*

On Sunday mornings after church or chapel some of the young putters and pony drivers would go to the drift stables and bring out the pit ponies to let them run loose in the field to the rear of Hazelgrove Terrace. The fun came when they had to catch them again to take them back to the stables situated down the mine.

The Fir Tree Football Team, 1903.
Image courtesy of Howden-le-Wear History Society

Life seemed to be hard, but it is what they were used to and they just got on with it as, when the call came, they did what they were asked to do. They joined up.

East End of Front Street, Fir Tree, 1914.
Image courtesy of Howden-le-Wear History Society.

Duke of York Inn and school, 1914.
Image courtesy of Howden-le-Wear History Society

Mr T. Finley, J.P., who lived in Fir Tree and was Managing Director of Harperley Collieries Company Ltd, was very generous to the men who served during the war in the armed forces who had worked for him. In early 1916, he established a war fund where each man in the colliery contributed 3 pence per week from his pay to be given for local war relief. The fund distributed sums varying from £5 upwards to £27 to the widows and dependants of those who died. The fund closed in 1919 after all the money was distributed.

Harperley Terrace, Fir Tree, 1914.
Image courtesy of Howden-le-Wear History Society

Roll of Honour

Stobart J G 2nd Lieutenant	3rd/6thBn.Attd 4thBn. Rifle Brigade	Killed in action 15th March 1915
Trathen T Pte 16828	6th Bn. Royal Scots Fusiliers	Declared missing 26th September 1915
McLeod A Pte	S/12773 Gordon Highlanders	Killed in action 14th January 1916
Kearton J Pte 4152	6th Bn. Durham Light Infantry	Died of wounds 23rd April 1916
Patton A Pte 16852	6th Bn. Royal Scots Fusiliers	Killed in action 30th May 1916
Vitty F Pte 14594	14th Bn. Durham Light Infantry	Declared missing 18th September1916
Wray J Pte 62976	6th Bn. Durham Light Infantry	Died of wounds 5th October 1917
Hoggarth E W **Pte** 204336	5th Bn. Durham Light Infantry	Died 4th August 1917
Fawcett C Pte 12037	Machine Gun Corps; Durham Light Infantry	Killed in action 22nd July 1917
Mosey J Pte 37892	Royal Berkshire Regiment	Declared missing 16th August 1917
Walkington J C **Pte** 22911	22nd Bn. Durham Light Infantry	Died of wounds 20th February 1918
Ramshaw J Pte 252407	6th Bn. Durham Light Infantry	Died of wounds 13th June 1918

John Geoffrey Stobart

2nd Lt. John Geoffrey Stobart, 6th D.L.I.

Image courtesy of John Alderson

Dorothy Stobart, Geoffrey's older sister, in the grounds of Harperley Hall c1900.

Image courtesy of Howden-le-Wear History Society

2nd Lieutenant John Geoffrey Stobart was born on the 28th January 1892 at Spellow Hill, Knaresborough, North Yorkshire, and was the son of William Culley Stobart and Frances Dorothea Wilkinson of Harperley Hall. He preferred to go by his middle name of 'Geoffrey' and he was educated at Aysgarth School, North Yorkshire. In the 1911 Census, it states he was a student at Cambridge attending Malvern and Pembroke Colleges. Geoffrey was a member of the Yorkshire Ramblers' Club, attending from 1910, and he became a full member in 1912, climbing Ben Nevis in the wildest of weather.

Geoffrey was a member of the Officer Training Corps at Cambridge and, at the outbreak of war, he volunteered for service and was attached to the 3rd Battalion Durham Light Infantry. 2nd Lieutenant Stobart was then assigned to the 6th Rifle Brigade when he was gazetted on probation on the 15th August 1914 at Sheerness, but was latterly attached to the 4th Battalion Rifle Brigade when he was deployed to France in February 1915.

Lieutenant Geoffrey Stobart was shot and killed whilst leading his platoon retaking trenches in the St Eloi area near to Ypres on the 15th March

1915, aged 23. He was buried at the Voormezeele Enclosure Cemetery No. 3 in Belgium. He is also remembered on the Fir Tree War Memorial and on a brass plaque in St Margaret of Antioch Church in Crossgate, Durham. The organ in the church was dedicated to the men of the Parish and congregation who laid down their lives during the Great War.

2nd Lieutenant Stobart was awarded the 1914/15 Star, the Victory Medal and the British War Medal, commonly being called, when all three were awarded together, "Pip, Squeak and Wilfred".

Thomas Trathen

In most of the records, his name is printed as Strathen, and this can be seen corrected on the War Memorial at Fir Tree. Thomas was the eldest son of Walter and Mary Trathen and was born in North Skelton, Yorkshire, in 1881. In the 1911 Census, they are shown as living as a family of ten at 8 Plantation Terrace, Fir Tree. At that time he was single, working down the local drift mine as a putter, alongside his father, a hewer, brother James, a fellow putter, and younger brother Richard, a pony driver.

Private Thomas Trathen enlisted as a volunteer, number 16828, in August 1914 and was attached to the newly formed 6th Service Battalion Royal Scots Fusiliers which formed at Ayr in Scotland as part of K1 in Kitchener's new army. They moved to Bordon for training and in February 1915 the battalion moved to Bramshott in Hampshire.

On the 11th May 1915, they landed on French soil at Bologne and four months later, on the 26th September 1915, Private Thomas Trathen was killed in action during the Battle of Loos, at the age of 34. The Battle of Loos was the largest British offensive of 1915 on the Western Front. In this battle, the British first used poison gas, and it was a massive engagement, attempting to break through the German defences and to take the fighting away from the stagnating trench warfare. The offensive failed despite the fact that the allies had more modern methods of warfare, more ammunition and better equipment. There was very heavy fighting and losses were high on both sides. On the morning of the 26th September, the 6th R.S.F, under the command of Major Turnbull, were surrounded on three sides by the German army and were under heavy shell fire. At the end of the day Private Trathen and many of his comrades were declared missing. He is remembered with honour on the Loos Memorial at Dud Corner Cemetery in France, on the Scottish War Memorial in Edinburgh Castle, and on the Fir Tree War Memorial.

His family later received his 1914/15 Star, the Victory Medal and the British War Medal, along with the death plaque.

Archibald McLeod

There are very few details available for Private McLeod other than the fact that his father was also called Archibald and his mother was Mary McLeod. He was born in Pencaitland, Haddingtonshire, just south east of Edinburgh. His father worked as a labourer in the Glenkinchie distillery. Archibald was married to Annie, and he was a farm labourer in 1901, and by 1914 he was living at Harperley Station.

Archibald volunteered and enlisted in the 1st Battalion of the Gordon Highlanders, number S/12773. He was posted to France on the 4th December 1915 and was killed in action some 43 days later on the 14th January 1916, at the age of 31. There were no major battles, but trench warfare would mean that he would be serving in the front line trenches enduring heavy artillery bombardment and many skirmishes with the enemy. It appears that four men from his company were killed on the same day, so it was highly possible that it was as a result of shell fire.

Private Archibald McLeod was buried with his four comrades at La Clytte Military Cemetery and a wooden cross was erected over his grave. This was replaced with a marker of Portland Stone after the war was over.

Private McLeod was awarded the 1914/15 Star, the Victory Medal and the British War Medal.

John Kearton

John Kearton was born at Muker in Swaledale in 1891 to John and Alice Kearton, where they had their own farm. It is believed that Alice moved the family to Fir Tree for work when her husband passed away. The family moved to Scur House, 2 Hazelgrove Terrace, Fir Tree, where she was head of the household in 1911, with John who was working as a coal miner 'hewer' in a local mine, alongside his two brothers James, a putter, and George, a pony driver.

When war broke out, John enlisted in the 2nd/6th Battalion of the Durham Light Infantry, also known as the Faithful Sixth. His army number was 4152. There are no military records available to show when John went to France, not even a Medal Roll Card, which is unusual.

John was wounded in one of the many battles around Ypres and was transferred back to England, being hospitalized locally at the Armstrong Hospital in Newcastle where, on the 23rd April 1916, he died of septic poisoning, aged 25. He was buried in St Mary's churchyard in Howden-le-Wear. There is no evidence of his family receiving his medal or death plaque, but he was probably awarded the 1914/15 Star, the Victory Medal and the British War Medal.

The grave of Private John Kearton, 6th DLI, in Howden-le-Wear churchyard. *Image courtesy of John Alderson*

Arthur Patton

Arthur Patton was born in 1892 in Fir Tree, Harperley. Arthur and his older sister Annie were brought up in the home of the grandfather, Robert Patton, in Fir Tree with their mother. No evidence of his mother's marriage was found, but Arthur and his sister had the surname Vickers for most of their life. His mother was also known as Mrs Vickers from 1901 onwards. In 1911, Arthur was living with his mother and a boarder in Fir Tree. His grandfather had presumably died and Isabelle was living 'on her own means'. Although Arthur was 19 at this time, he had no known occupation.

Jutland Cottage, Fir Tree, where the Patton family lived.
Image courtesy of Howden-le-Wear History Society

The records show that Arthur enlisted not as Arthur Vickers, but as Arthur Patton, and his mother was also known as Mrs Patton. He enlisted at Bishop Auckland and arrived in France on the 31st July 1915 serving with the 6th Battalion of the Royal Scots Fusiliers, army number 16852.

Arthur would have seen action during the Battle of Loos in September and October 1915 and is reported to have been killed in action on the 30th May 1916. He was buried at Vermelles British Cemetery in northern France. Arthur was awarded the 1914/15 Star, the Victory Medal and the British War Medal.

Fred Vitty

Fred was born in 1897 to William and Priscilla Vitty at Wheatley Hill. When they moved to 10 Institute Terrace, Fir Tree, they did so to work for

Harperley Collieries. His father William was a hewer, his brother George was a putter, and Fred became a pony driver. He also joined one of the first scout troops in the north east in 1910, formed by his father William and his friend Robert Baden Powell.

Scoutmaster William Vitty and a group of Fir Tree boy scouts, 1911.
Image courtesy of John Alderson

On the 8th September 1914, Fred and George walked to Howden-le-Wear and boarded the train for Bishop Auckland. On arrival at the recruiting office, they signed their Attestation Papers. Fred lied about his age as he was only 17 and stated that he was born in 1895. The description on the papers states that he had sallow skin, grey eyes and light brown hair. By the 9th September, they were in barracks at Newcastle where they joined the other recruits of the 14th Durham Light Infantry.

On the 24th they marched through Newcastle and boarded the train to take them to Aylesbury in Buckinghamshire, the first time the Vitty brothers had ever left the north east. When they arrived in Aylesbury there was no actual camp, but they were provided with tents, and on the 3rd October they moved again to Halton Park as part of Lord Kitchener's New 3rd Army.

Training began in earnest and on the 27th November they moved to billets in High Wycombe where they stayed all winter.

14th DLI training at Halton Camp, 1915.

Image courtesy of John Alderson

Band members of "D" Company, 14th DLI at Halton Camp in 1915.

Image courtesy of John Alderson

In the spring, they returned to Halton Park and then in July they moved to Whitley in Surrey to be mobilized for war. They landed at Boulogne in France on the 11th September 1915 and within three days they were fighting near Nielles-Les-Ardres. The brothers were involved in nine different engagements around this area for the next few months in and out of the line.

These men were moving forward and fighting in horrendous conditions: mud, water, being shot at, shrapnel, shell fire, gas, lack of sleep, sleeping in the open where possible, machine gun fire. As well as all of this they had to carry a steel helmet, haversack on their back, water bottle filled, entrenching tool, waterproof sheet, gas helmet, box respirator, 2 sand bags, 2 grenades, 120 rounds S.A.A., 2 flares, 1 iron ration, 1 day's preserved meat & biscuits, field dressing.

Private Fred Vitty, 14th Battalion DLI.

Image courtesy of John Alderson

On top of this every man carried a large tool on his back at a proportion of 5 shovels to 2 picks. Lewis gunners and signallers also carried their own equipment, wire cutters, Very pistols and cartridges, and S.O.S. rockets. And they left the Durham coal mines for this?

On the night of the 17th December, Fred, George and 5 other members of "D" Company left the line just south of Wieltje on an intelligence gathering mission towards the German line. They ended up being caught in no-man's-land for the next few days, hiding in shell craters and old trenches, being shot at by both Germans and the British. On the morning of the 19th at about 5.30am, a greenish-yellow cloud of phosgene gas swept across the battle field from the German line and, under heavy shell fire, they reached for their gas hoods. George, finding that his hood was full of holes, as did another two, they reached for their whistles and ran for their own front line blowing fiercely and diving into their trenches. George was evacuated to a field ambulance station for first aid treatment.

The 14th DLI bore the brunt of the gas attack that day as they were in low lying ground. The men of "D" Company had to keep their gas hoods on for five hours while still standing to in case of a German attack following the shelling.

The 14th DLI took part in approximately ten further major offensives before September 12th when they were moved from Sand Pitt Valley to the Citadel to the south of Fricourt where the 14th made their first appearance on the Somme battlefield. They made their way to the front line to fight and also to re-dig and repair trenches, and to move the wounded and the dead of the Norfolk and Suffolk Regiments.

In the early hours of the 18th September they suffered a heavy and hostile German artillery barrage and it was during this bombardment that Private Fred Vitty, number 14594, lost his life. To this day he is still one of the unknown. He is remembered on the Thiepval Memorial. Private Vitty had served the colours for 2 years and 11 days and lost his life at the age of 19 years. Private Fred Vitty was awarded the 1914/15 Star, the Victory Medal and the British War Medal. He is also remembered on the Boy Scout Roll of Honour (page 314). An allowance was awarded to his mother Priscilla of 3s 6d (approximately 17 new pence) each week.

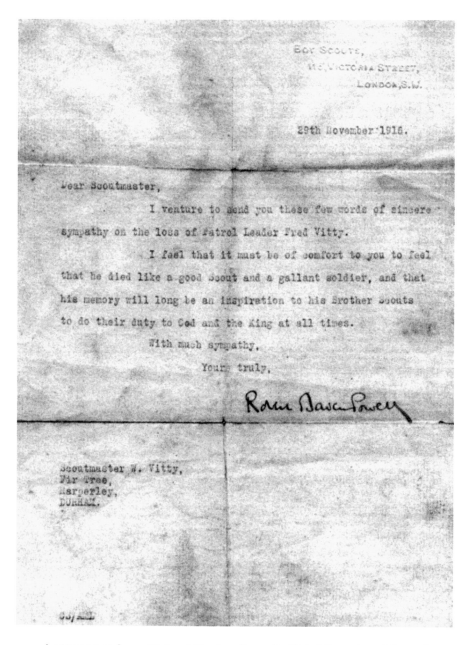

Boy Scouts,
116, Victoria Street,
London, S.W.

29th November 1916.

Dear Scoutmaster,

I venture to send you these few words of sincere
sympathy on the loss of Patrol Leader Fred Vitty.

I feel that it must be of comfort to you to feel
that he died like a good Scout and a gallant soldier, and that
his memory will long be an inspiration to his Brother Scouts
to do their duty to God and the King at all times.

With much sympathy.

Yours truly,

Robert Baden Powell

Scoutmaster W. Vitty,
Fir Tree,
Harperley,
DURHAM.

Letter sent from Robert Baden Powell, Chief Scout and founder of the Boy Scout movement, to his friend William Vitty, Scoutmaster of Fir Tree, in condolence on the death of his son Fred.

Image courtesy of John Alderson

Private Alfred Calton wrote the poem 'Division Forty Nine' after he saved the life of Private George Vitty and many others during the phosgene gas attack on the 19th December 1915. He was serving with the 1st Battalion of the West Yorkshire Regiment.

Approximately 13 months later, at the age of 21, Private Alfred Calton, number 26959, lost his life on the 26th January 1917, near Bethune. He was buried in Bethune Town Cemetery.

"Division Forty Nine"

'Twas the break of dawn in Flanders and the morning promised bright,
The nineteenth of December and a lovely day to fight;
The Forty-Ninth Division got orders to "stand to"
But little did they know just what they were going to do.

At five o'clock exactly, the sentry gave a start,
For just beyond he saw a sight which touched his softening heart;
'Twas the greenish fumes of Phosgene gas, and those awful deadly fumes,
Were sweeping towards our lines to send men to their dooms,

The men kept splendid order when they heard the gas gong sound,
To fix all smoke helmets, the order soon went round;
But some had been too slow to heed, or their helmets had mislaid,
And as the gas fumes caught them, each one a victim made.

Then the guns began to thunder, and the shells began to burst,
Each victim of the deadly gas, was seized with awful thirst;
But drinks were out of question, for water was not nigh,
And so they lay down in the trench, to gasp, and choke, and die.

But the rest stuck to it bravely, as they manned each trench and sap,
They did not mean to let the Huns fill up one single gap;
Then we "Medics" got the order, we are needed right away,
And fearful were the sights we saw that eventful day.

There was no volunteering, for not a man delay,
For picking our smoke helmets up, we dashed upon parade;
We were hurried to the trenches, to get the sick away,
And midst a hail of bursting shells we had to work all day.

We did our duty willingly, no order did we shirk,
We knew it was our duty, and 'twas good and noble work;
And when our work at last was done, it seemed so strange to me,
To hear the infantry cry out: "Well done. R.A.M.C."

And these are Territorials, Division Forty Nine,
Who though very short in numbers, still held the British line,

And there they've been for just six months, in water, mud and ice,
But still they've held the German hordes as if 'twere in a vice.

There's many a mother in England will oft have prayed to God,
To take the soul of her dear son, who lies beneath the sod,
There's many a lonely widow, whose husband she now knows,
Lies 'neath the soil in Belgium, near where the Yser flows.

But the day is drawing nearer, for the "Yorkshire Boys'"' return,
When the guns have ceased to thunder and they get the rest they've earned;
They will soon be leaving Flanders and coming o'er the foam,
So prepare a good reception, when the boys come marching home.'

Written by Private A. Calton of the 2nd West Yorkshire Regiment
on the 21st December 1915.

John Wray

John Wray was born in 1896, son of Thomas and Mary Jane Wray of The Lodge, Farfield, Buttershaw, Bradford, in Yorkshire, and in 1911 John, his parents and his three younger sisters were living at East Lodge, Harperley Park. John was working as a driver in a local coal mine.

John enlisted with the 6th Durham Light Infantry and at that time his enlistment address was still at Harperley Park.

John disembarked in France with the 6th Durham Light Infantry on the 27th June 1915 with the number 62976. John saw immediate front line action and he died from wounds received in battle on the 5th October 1916 at the age of 20. Also on that day Lieutenant C. Catford of the 1st Battalion DLI was killed and buried with Private Wray and 14 other men who died that day in Dernancourt Communal Cemetery Extension. He was awarded the 1914/15 Star, the Victory Medal and the British War Medal.

Edward William Hoggarth

Edward William Hoggarth was baptised on the 3rd December 1886 in Crook and was the son of James and Elizabeth Hoggarth. He had three sisters, Rebecca, Hannah and Agnes. Edward married Annie Gibson on the 2nd December 1912 at Bishop Auckland Registry Office.

Private Edward William Hoggarth, army number 204336, enlisted in "B" Company of the 5th Battalion of the Durham Light Infantry on the 19th February 1916 at Stockton. His address at the time of enlistment was 11 Fir Tree, Harperley, and his occupation was that of a cartman. His attestation stated that he was 27 years and 3 months of age, but in fact was 29 years old. He was also 6 ft 4 ins tall. He was transferred to the Army Reserve the following day. This was possibly because his fitness level was not of a high enough level for active service.

Private Edward Hoggarth was mobilised on the 31st May 1917, but was admitted to Catterick Military Hospital on the 6th June 1917 with a condition affecting his urinary tract. He was seriously ill and by the 29th June was dangerously ill with high fever. His condition improved over the next week and on the 3rd July he was recorded as being 'out of danger'. Edward's condition suddenly deteriorated during the early hours of the 4th July and, despite emergency treatment by the medical staff, he died at 3.35am of heart and renal failure.

The attending medical officer, Dr George Longstaff, stated in Edward's records:

> 'I am of the opinion that Private Hoggarth's condition was not caused or aggravated by military service'.

This comment would affect the amount of pension that Annie would receive and she was awarded a service pension of 13s 9d a week from the 21st January 1918. This was withdrawn when she later moved to 1 Amblers Terrace, Close House, Bishop Auckland, and married a Mr W. Hudson.

Private Edward Hoggarth's army service lasted for 35 days and his body was returned to County Durham and he was buried at Crook cemetery.

There is no evidence that Edward was awarded the Victoria and British War Medal, but Annie was sent a memorial scroll and a death plaque on the 4th May 1920.

Charles Fawcett

Charles Fawcett was born in 1890 to William and Elizabeth Fawcett of Tanfield Lee, Tantobie, County Durham. In the 1911 Census, Charles is recorded as living at 5 King Edward Street, Tanfield Lea, and was working as an above ground colliery labourer. His father and older brother Horatio were colliery blacksmiths and his brother John was a railway engineman. They also had a housekeeper living in the home with them as Charles's mother had died.

It is believed that after 1911, Charles moved to work for Harperley Collieries and lodged in Fir Tree through the week.

Private Charles Fawcett enlisted in the Northumberland Fusiliers, with army number 22642, and later transferred to 54th Company Machine Gun Corps (Infantry) where his army number was 12037.

He was fighting in the area around Arras when he was wounded and killed on the 22nd July 1917 at the age of 27. He was buried in the Lijssenthoek Military Cemetery and was awarded the Victory Medal and the British War Medal. Charles is named on the War Memorial in Fir Tree and also on the memorial in the Methodist Chapel at Tanfield Lea.

Jonathan Mosey

Jonathan (sometimes spelt as Johnathan in records) was born in 1898 at New Kyo near to Anfield Plain in County Durham, son of George and Mary Jane Mosey. His father was a miner trolleyway man and had been born in Hamilton Row. The 1911 Census states that Jonathan was still at school and was 12 years of age. He had seven siblings.

From other records, it is believed that his father came to work for Harperley Collieries and that Jonathan was working with him when he lied about his age to enlist in the Durham Light Infantry with the number 23169 at the age of 16. He transferred to the 2nd Battalion of the Princess Charlotte of Wales' Royal Berkshire Regiment and was given the number of 37892.

Private Mosey arrived in France on the 11th September 1915 and transferred to the Royal Berkshires. He was reported missing in action on 16th August 1917 and is remembered on the Tyne Cot Memorial. His home address was recorded at the time as being 28 First Street, South Moor, Stanley, Co. Durham.

He was awarded the 1914/15 Star, the Victory Medal and the British War Medal.

John Cooper Walkington

John Walkington was born to William and Annie Walkington in 1891 at Bishop Wilton, Yorkshire. He had two brothers, Herbert and Frederick, and a sister Dora. In 1911, his occupation was a horseman on a farm.

John moved to Fir Tree and was working as a colliery banksman at Woodifield Colliery and was living at High Woodifield, Crook, when he enlisted in the Durham Light Infantry on the 11th December 1915. John had some problems with his ears and was placed on the medical reserve list until this problem had cleared up. He was mobilised on the 11th February 1916 and served with the 22nd Durham Light Infantry (Pioneer Corps). He was 5 ft 2 ins tall and had a chest measurement of 35 ins. His army number was 22/911.

Private John Walkington served in France from the 6th June 1916. He was given home leave from the 19th - 28th September 1917 when he married Annie Cooper in Bishop Auckland. They set up home at 3 Coronation Terrace, Fir Tree. John rewrote his will to leave everything to his wife and she was awarded a separation allowance of 12s 6d a week.

John returned to France within days of their marriage and died of his wounds on the 20th February 1918 at the Somme Redoubt. He was buried at Ypres Reservoir Cemetery. Annie was awarded a widow's pension of 13s 9d a week from the 2nd September 1918.

Annie was sent John's Victory Medal and British War Medal after she had remarried to a Mr Alf Gowland, and they lived at 10 West Road, Crook.

Joseph Ramshaw

Joseph Ramshaw was born in Stanley, County Durham, in 1892. He was the oldest son of Robert and Annie Ramshaw and he had one brother and three sisters. By 1911 Joseph was lodging at Billy Row, and was working in a Fir Tree Drift mine as a putter.

In April 1914, Joseph married Florence Vitty of 10 Institute Terrace, Fir Tree. He enlisted at Bishop Auckland in the September at approximately the same time his two brothers-in-law, George and Fred Vitty.

Private Joseph Ramshaw with army number 252407, joined the 1st/6th Battalion of the Durham Light Infantry.

He landed in France on the 20th April 1915, and was wounded in May 1918. Joseph was brought back to Fir Tree where he died, aged 26, on the 13th June 1918 at his home in 11 Institute Terrace, Fir Tree.

Joseph was buried in St Mary's churchyard, Howden-le-Wear, and is remembered on the Fir Tree War Memorial. His wife later received his 1914/15 Star, the Victory Medal and the British War Medal.

Private Joseph Ramshaw, 6th Battalion DLI.
Image courtesy of John Alderson

"They shall grow not old as we that are left grow old: Age shall not weary them, nor the years condemn. At the going down of the sun and in the morning We will remember them."

"We will Remember Them"

'Ode to Remembrance'

The War Memorial

The War Memorial was erected in July 1921 in memory of the men of Fir Tree who gave their lives. It took the form of a handsome drinking fountain erected on land given by Mr T. Hird in the centre of the village.

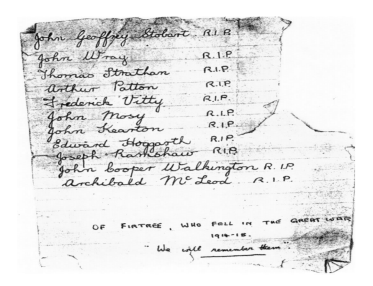

Copy of the original list of names for those mentioned on the War Memorial at Fir Tree, 1914 - 1918 War.

Image courtesy of Howden-le-Wear History Society

Fir Tree men sitting around the memorial which originally was a water fountain.

Image courtesy of Howden-le Wear History Society

The Fir Tree War Memorial in its original location in the early 1920s. It was later moved farther along the road to allow for new buildings to be erected.

Image courtesy of Howden-le-Wear History Society

The War Memorial was later moved to a new position where it can still be viewed in all its grandeur and elegance.

Fir Tree War Memorial. *Image courtesy of www.geograph.org.uk*

THE WAR TO END ALL WARS

The Armistice was finally signed on the 11th November 1918 and the Peace was declared with the signing of the Treaty of Versailles on the 28th June 1919. The Great War had left Europe devastated. The countries suffered casualties never experienced before:

Britain: 750,000 soldiers killed; 1,500,000 wounded
France: 1,400,000 soldiers killed; 2,500,000 wounded
Belgium: 50,000 soldiers killed
Italy: 600,000 soldiers killed
Russia: 1,700,000 soldiers killed
America: 116,000 soldiers killed

The Central Powers also suffered heavy casualties:

Germany: 2,000,000 soldiers killed
Austria-Hungary: 1,200,000 soldiers killed
Turkey: 325,000 soldiers killed
Bulgaria: 100,000 soldiers killed

The total deaths of all nations who fought in the war were thought to have been over 8.5 million, with 21 million men wounded.

Alongside these statistics was the fact that vast areas of northern Europe had been reduced to rubble. Flanders had been all but destroyed, with the ancient city of Ypres being amongst many which had been devastated. The homes of 750,000 French people were decimated and the infrastructure severely damaged. Roads, coal mines and telegraph poles had all been destroyed and such a loss greatly hindered the area's ability to return to normality.

During mid-1918 until 1920, Europe was hit by Spanish flu and an estimated 40 million people died worldwide, many of whom were the youth and young people who survived the fighting. This added to the desolation felt by many, and it took many years for the countries, victors and vanquished alike, to restore their faith in human nature and feel that this war was the 'War to end all Wars'.

Sadly it was not to be.

❖ *ONE HUNDRED YEARS ON*

One hundred years on, there are relatives of many of these men still living in and around the villages of Fir Tree and Howden-le-Wear. Some still talk of what their grandparents or great grandparents used to do and how they lived. Others are intrigued by what the village was like in the past; by the local mining industry; the cricket and football teams; where children played and went to school; how the local industry developed and then declined and disappeared; and what was left of the seggar heaps.

The 100th anniversary of the start of the Great War in 2014 has focused the minds of many to reflect on the lives of local people of 100 years ago.   All the people who have contributed to this book have found it a very moving and cathartic experience, and hope that the legacy of the men and their families has been restored.

❖ *Appendix I*

ABSENT VOTERS' LIST FROM HOWDEN-LE-WEAR OCTOBER 1918

The Absent Voters' List 1918 was produced to encourage men serving with the colours to vote in the 1918 General Election to boost the electorate actually placing their vote. The details were supplied by the next of kin of the soldiers to local registration officers who forwarded the information to the War Office. Voting cards and ballot papers were sent to soldiers serving in France, Flanders and Italy. Men serving further afield voted through a proxy voting form. The collation of the information was hurried and haphazard and often men were missed off the list or inaccurate details were given by the family.

Being aware of the issues with the Absent Voters' List of October 1918, it is one of the few ways which provides a comprehensive list of the names of the servicemen from specific areas, the majority of whom did return to their communities after the conflict.

The men from Howden-le-Wear district are named as follows:

Adamson, John	42 Low Beechburn, Crook	245159 Pte, att. ELB
Adamson, Frank	42 Middle Row, Low Beechburn	78773 Pte, 4th Res Northumberland Fusiliers
Aisbett, Ambrose	The Square, Howden-le-Wear	2nd B Section, Royal Engineers
Aldworth, Wilfred	69 High Flat, Crook	32680 Royal Field Artillery
Allport, John	65 High Street, Howden-le-Wear	116055 A/M, 5th TDS, R.A.F.
Askew, David	65 High Street, Howden-le-Wear	38549 Pte, 20th DLI

**Private George Binks
who fought the Turks
in the Middle East with
with the Army Service
Corps.**
*Image courtesy of
Auckland Chronicle*

**Private David Askew,
of the Durham Light
Infantry who survived
the war but spent
much of it as a
prisoner of war in
Germany .**
*Image courtesy of
Auckland Chronicle*

Both men survived the war and returned home to Howden-le-Wear.

Bains, Douglas	The Hollow, nr Crook	222332 Gunner, D 107th BDE, Royal Field Artillery
Bains, Thomas Harold	The Hollow, nr Crook	240547, 2/4th Yorks and Lancs
Battensby, Henry	9 Wear Valley Junction	22089, Sgt. R.A.M.C.
Bell, Ernest	White House, Howden-le-Wear	95499, Pte. 5th Durham Light Infantry
Bell, George	41 Low Beechburn, Crook	195769, Gunner, Tynemouth Royal Garrison Artillery
Binks, George Henry	16 High Street, Howden-le-Wear	T4/042788 , Corp. 249th Coy, Army Service Corp
Boon, Walter	20 Church St, Howden-le-Wear	043162 Army Service Corp
Bowsfield, Alfred	West View, Howden-le-Wear	02162 Corporal, Army Ordinance Corp
Bouson	Howden-le-Wear	34777 Pte 1st F.G.G.S. Staffordshire Regiment
Bramwell, Thomas Wm	22 Church St, Howden-le-Wear	17113, Pte Yorks Regiment
Bretton, Thomas	8 Bridge St, Howden-le-Wear	217241, 61st Wing R.A.F.
Britton, Thomas Henry	26 High St, Howden-le-Wear	M2/168015 (MT) Army Service Corp

Broadbent, James	1 Victoria	245169, Pte. R.E.
Brothers, Alfred	14 Hayill, Rd, Howden-le-Wear	751159 Gunner Royal Field Artillery
Browell, George	30 Victoria	365757, Par., Tyne Electrical Engineers, R.E.
Brown, Alfred Matthew Henry	Myrtle House, 30 Hargill Bank, Howden-le-Wear	5933/155 Able Seaman, NK, MN, RNB, Portsmouth
Brown, George	30 Victoria	03361 Pte. A.O.C.
Brown Hubert	Brookside, Crook	235774 Pte, Reserve Btn, West Yorkshire Regiment
Brown, Joseph Wm	27 Hayill Rd, Howden-le-Wear	58058 141st Royal Army Medical Corp
Brown, Peter	Myrtle House, 30 Hargill Bank, Howden-le-Wear	13835 Durham Light Infantry
Brown, William Franklin	13 Victoria St, Howden-le-Wear	2659 Pte. 6th DLI

Carr, Ralph	55 High St, Howden-le-Wear	74123 Pte. 4th Coy, 3rd DLI
Calvert, Ernest Edward	26 High St, Howden-le-Wear	DLI
Calvert, Joseph Monkhouse	Beechwood, Howden-le-Wear	MT, Army Service Corp
Charles, John William	46 Valley Terrace	123713 Bdr. R.G.A.
Chopping, George	11 Victoria	6649 50thm Sgd. R.T.S. A.S.C.
Cole, Frederick	Prospect Pl. Howden-le-Wear	2nd Lieut. Royal Lancashire Regiment
Cole, Wilfred	Prospect Pl. Howden-le-Wear	51507 Pte. 11th West Yorkshire Regiment
Collingwood, Fred	16 Railway Ter, Wear Valley Junction	342569 Sap. 1st Res R.F
Collins, Robert Fairless	47 Low Beechburn, Crook	698 Pte. 11th DLI
Carrick, Louis	17 Greenhead, Crook	562838 Pte. 682 Agric. Coy. Labour Corp.
Collier, Wm. Walton	Bridge St, Howden-le-Wear	1/4/008918 Dvr. 799th Coy. Army Service Corp.
Cook, John Henry	Station House, Beechburn	239479 Dvr. 158th BAC Royal Field Artillery
Corner, Frederick	39 Valley Terrace	TR/5/186281 Pte 116the T.R.B.
Corner, George Alfred	39 Valley Terrace	45680 Pte. 15th DLI
Cousin, Alexander	Plantation Tce. Howden-le-Wear	39824 Pte 2nd Res. Cav. Regt
Cousin, Matthew	46 Low Beechburn, Crook	277309 7th DLI
Cousin, Thomas Chas.	Sunnydene, Howden-le-Wear	100029 Bdr. 221st Siege Bat. Royal Garrison Artillery
Crabtree, James	52 Victoria	67641, Pte. R.D.C.

Davies, James William	31 Victoria	8th DLI
Dobson, Herbert Henry	5 Bridge St, Howden-le-Wear	Durham Light Infantry
Doyle, Arthur	60 Low Beechburn, Crook	771765 Dvr, Royal Field Artillery
Dent, Matthew	High Farm, Crook	236879 Pte, 412 Agric. Coy. Labour Corp
Dixon, Harry	c/o Mrs Shorton, High St, Howden-le-Wear	270063 Pte, 18th Durham Light Infantry
Dyson, Alan	Hayill Rd, Howden-le-Wear	8366 Cadet, 12th OTB
Dyson, Norman	Church St, Howden-le-Wear	15924 Pte Coldstream Guards.

Elliot, Robert Michael	18 High St, Howden-le-Wear	Pte, A Coy. 2/6th Manchester Regiment.
English, Herbert	5 School St, Howden-le-Wear	PO/S/884 Pte end R.M. Bn. RND
Ellis, John Spouage	7 Bridge St, Howden-le-Wear	35577 Pte, 7th Bn Gloucester Regiment
Fenton, Edward	29 Stable Row, Greenhead, Crook	464 Pte 19th Durham Light Infantry
Fenton, John Thomas	29 Stable Row, Greenhead, Crook	8827
Follon, Daniel	31 Victoria	26/900 Pte. 12/13th N.F.
Foster, Arthur Peverell	Church St. Howden-le-Wear	20868 Pte 23rd Cycle Brigade
Foster, Frederick	7 Victoria	909994 Pte. Garrison, A.G. Guards
Frazer, John George	Whitfield Cottages, Crook	52422 Royal Garrison Artillery, Heavy Repair Shop
Fryer, Gatenby	4 Garden Pl. Howden-le-Wear	N/348921 Pte. Army Service Corp, 1081 MT Coy.
Fulcher, Thomas Wm	15 Church St, Howden-le-Wear	554831 Pte. 360th Res. Employ. Coy.

Gibson, Joseph	28 Long Row, Beechburn	372751 Mortar T.A.S
Gray, Emmerson Walton	20 Stable Row, Greenhead, Crook	205521 Pte. 10th Bn. R.W.K.R.
Gill, Frederick Roger	59 Low Beechburn, Crook	103166 Cpl 24 Sta. Hospital. Royal Army Medical Corp
Gill, James Henry	1 Chapel Row, Greenhead, Crook	206229 Gunner A Siege Dept. Royal Garrison Artillery
Glover, George	25 Valley Terrace	408523 Pte. 23rd Garrison A.G. Guards
Goodwin, Albert	35 Victoria	31972 Pte. 2nd DLI
Haley, Thomas	50 Valley Terrace	74091 Pte. 2nd DLI
Hansom, John Henry	67 High St, Howden-le-Wear	30808 Pte 827th Employ Coy.
Hansom, Gilbert	56 High St, Howden-le-Wear	83656 Pte. 4th Res. Northumberland Fusiliers

Hardy, Donald	26 Valley Terrace	12854 Spr, R.E.
Hardy, John Thomas	59 Victoria Cottages	205248 Pte. 1/6th DLI
Hardy, Wilfred	The Hollow, Crook	102877 178th Coy. Royal Engineers
Harrison, George	12 Railway Tce, Wear Valley Junction	269295 Spr, R.O.D. R.E.
Hart, John Joseph	Bridge St, Howden-le-Wear	37410 Pte. Kings Own Yorkshire Light Infantry
Hauxwell, James Wm	The Hollow, Crook	7222 Pte Sherwood Forresters
Hauxwell, John	The Hollow, Crook	18720 Pte 13th Durham Light Infantry
Hewitt, Joseph	29 Low Beechburn, Crook	Pte. Durham Light Infantry
Hill, William Thompson	15 The Hollow, nr Crook	251898 Dvr. Royal Field Artillery
Holloway, Spence	13 Chapel Row, Greenhead,	250402 Pte. 6th DLI
Hunter, John Edward	Hargill Road, Howden-le-Wear	16935 Pte 10th Hampshire Regiment
Hurst, Percy	28 Victoria	24916 Pte. 13th Coldstream Guards
Hutchinson, William	18 Low Road, Beechburn	95467 Pte. 5th Durham Light Infantry
Hutchinson, Percy Clifton	28 Victoria Cottages	21344, Sgt. R.A.M.C 62nd General Hospital

Jackson, Thomas	Salmon House, Howden-le-Wear	454702 Pte. 415th Agric. Coy
Johnson, Henry	38 Victoria	337924 Cpl 550th Siege Batt. R.G.A.
Johnson, Ralph	9 Hargill Road, Howden-le-Wear	459129 3rd AM R.A.F.
Johnson, Robert	38 Victoria	148248 Pte M.G.C.
Jordan, John Ralph	Hargill Rd, Howden-le-Wear	127279 Gnr. 51st Siege Batt. Royal Garrison Artillery
Key, John George	31 Victoria	95048 Pte. 4th DLI
Key, Thomas	50 Victoria Cot. Howden-le-Wear	91339 Pte. 8th Durham Light Infantry

Lamb, Matthew	High Farm, Beechburn	Unknown
Lancaster, Joseph Lancelot	Ivy House, The Hollow, Crook	73945 Pte. A Coy. 4th Bn. Durham Light Infantry
Lawson, Frederick	44 High St, Howden-le-Wear	403825 Pte/ 4th Labour Corp
Lawson, Alfred Wm	Thistle Flat Farm, Crook	J62539 Able Seaman, RNB Portsmouth
Layton, Joseph	5 Wear Valley Junction	42925 Pte. 6th Line Regiment
Lee, John	51 High St, Howden-le-Wear	95041 Pte 4th Durham Light Infantry
Lee, Henry	16 Hargill Rd, Howden-le-Wear	96212 Pte. 4th Res Bn. Gloucester Infantry

Ling, Harry Rush	Howden-le-Wear	G/6840 Pte. End Bn. The Buffs.
Luck, Robert Henry	Low Beechburn, Crook	103118 Pte. 24th Italy Hospital, Royal Army Medical Corp
Lynas, Andrew	11 Railway St. Howden-le-Wear	205762 Pte. 11th East Yorkshire Regt.

McAdam, Samuel	53 Victoria	104502 Gnr. R.G.A.
Metcalf, Sydney	Violet Tce, Howden-le-Wear	316132 Pte. I.W.D. Royal Engineers
Moses, William	Bridge St, Howden-le-Wear	30067 Pte. B Coy. 1st East Yorkshire Regiment
Nicholson, Albert	49 Valley Terrace	9771 Rflmn. 7th Batt. Rifle Brigade
Norman, Arthur	58 Victoria	15006 Pte. 4th E. Yorks Regt.
Nutley, Harold Pearson	Hargill Rd, Howden-le-Wear	51406 L/Cpl 1st Lincoln Regiment

Parkin, Joseph	39 High St, Howden-le-Wear	ADC Remounts, Overseas Sqd.
Parker, William	2 Holly St, Howden-le-Wear	14th Coldstream Guards
Parkinson, George	7 High St, Howden-le-Wear	19360 Pte East Yorkshire Regiment
Parkinson, Robert	7 High St, Howden-le-Wear	16692 Pte East Yorkshire Regiment
Patterson, John	17 High St, Howden-le-Wear	82770 Pte Royal Army Medical Corp.
Peart, Watson	Hargill Rd. Howden-le-Wear	Pte. Kings Own Yorkshire Light Infantry
Pinkney, Henry Ernest	54 High St. Howden-le-Wear	35344 Pte 12/13th Northumberland Fusiliers
Peel, Joseph Henry	14 School St, Howden-le-Wear	285770 Sapper, 3rd Coy. Durham Fortress, Royal Engineers
Phillipson, John Watson	16 High St, Howden-le-Wear	261600 Sapper, 641 North F A Coy. Royal Engineers
Price, Matthew	Greenhead, near Crook	24/873 Pte. 22nd Bn Northumberland Fusiliers
Ramsdale, Ralph Nicholas	15 Wear Valley Junction	WR271436 Sapper, 22L Railway TR. CW. Royal Engineers
Robinson, Charles	The Hollow, near Crook	04992 2nd Cpl. A.O.C.
Ramsdale, Roland	15 Wear Valley Junction	236550 Spr R.E.
Richardson, Joseph S	11 Wear Valley Junction	S.M.88991 R.A.M.C.
Robson, William	67 High Flat, Crook	19578 Pte. APWO Yorks

Robson, Joseph	54 Low Beechburn, Crook	39997 Pte. 7th Yorks and Lancs.
Robson, John Edward Holliday	Ivy Cottage, Low Beechburn	770562 Northumberland R.A.
Ross, Henry	13 Victoria Row	203348 L.Cpl. 20th DLI
Ryan, Edward	60 High St, Howden-le-Wear	250049 Pte 6th Durham Light Infantry
Raine, John James	Church St, Howden-le-Wear	39823 Pte Cav.

Samuels, John	Church St, Howden-le-Wear	28551 Pte. 7th RDF
Sanderson, John	Hargill Rd, Howden-le-Wear	92963 Sapper, 30th Airline Sec. Royal Engineers
Sanderson, John	23 Victoria Terrace	770179 Driver, 321st R.F.A.
Sanderson, Nichol	The Hollow, near Crook	40618, Pte 5th Durham Light Infantry
Stephenson, Arthur Lawrence	2 Station Rd, Howden-le-Wear	377 Pioneer Sergt. 22nd Durham Light Infantry
Scott, Archibald	The Hollow, near Crook	G/80921 Pte. 1st Res. London Regiment
Scott, George	46 Valley Terrace	25401 Pte, 14th Coldstream Guards
Sleights, Albert	20 Victoria	273092 Pte. 6th DLI
Sleights, Thomas	20 Victoria	48479 Pte, 3rd Yorks
Sleights, William	20 Victoria	470380 Pte. 4th DLI
Stephenson, Geo.	27 Stable Row, Greenhead	271238 Pte Royal Scots
Stockdale, William	Chapel Row, Greenhead	20473 Pte 8th Northumberland Fusiliers
Tarn, George Bradley	8 High St, Howden-le-Wear	379 Pioneer Corporal, 22nd Durham Light Infantry
Tarn, John Thomas	8 High St, Howden-le-Wear	31211 Bandsman, 2nd Durham Light Infantry
Tarn, William Gladstone	8 High St, Howden-le-Wear	31387 Pte. 22nd Durham Light Infantry
Taylor, Archibald H	57 Valley Terrace	95454 Pte. 5th Res. DLI
Thompson, John	Hargill Rd, Howden-le-Wear	1104 DVr. Trans. Sec. 22nd Durham Light Infantry
Thompson, Joseph	27 Stable Row, Greenhead	250303 Pte 6th Durham Light Infantry
Turnbull, Robert Wm.	20 Bridge St, Howden-le-Wear	201029 Pte. 20th Durham Light Infantry
Thompson, William	Bridge House, Howden-le-Wear	24458 Pte. 41st Labour Coy.
Trennery, Joseph Wm.	Park View, Howden-le-Wear	91840 Royal Army Medical Corp
Trimble, Owen	17 Victoria	100267 Pte. 5th Red DLI
Turnbull, John Matthew	20 Bridge St, Howden-le-Wear	205669 Pte. Northumberland Fusiliers
Tweddle, James Wm.	7 Holly Tce. Howden-le-Wear	316395 Pte. Northumberland Fusiliers

Walton, Percy	Bridge St, Howden-le-Wear	67596 Pte. X coy. 2nd Bn Royal Fusiliers
Walton, Percy	1 High St, Howden-le-Wear	9018 Royal Army Medical Corp
Walton, Walter	1 High St, Howden-le-Wear	43480 Pte. Durham Light Inf. Inf.
Weatherald, Anthony	Hargill Rd, Howden-le-Wear	715 B Coy. N.E.R. Bn. Pioneers
Whitton, Dennis	29 Victoria	50873 Gnr R.G.A.
Whitton, George	29 Victoria	72609 Gnt. 54th Bde. R.F.A.
Winter, Albert	63 High St, Howden-le-Wear	515597 Pte 99th Labour Corp
Williams, John Rowe	Victoria Row	216736 Gnr. R.G.A
Whincup, Walter	12 Chapel Row, Greenhead	315th Road Construction Coy, Royal Engineers
Wilson, George Frederick	Hampden House, Howden-le-Wear	030634 Pte. Sec 18. Army Ordinance Corp
Wilson, George	Low Beechburn, Crook	203250 Pte 6th Res. Duke of Wellington Regiment
Wood, Alfred	68 High St. Howden-le-Wear	201944 Pte Scottish Rifles
Wood, Frederick	68 High St. Howden-le-Wear	93591 Pte. Royal Army Medical Corp
Young, John Edward	High St, Howden-le-Wear	023734 Army Ordinance Corp.
Young, William	1 Park Terrace	225 Pte. R.A.M.C

❖ *Appendix II*

THE SURVIVORS FROM FIR TREE

Wounded soldiers raising money in Institute Terrace, Fir Tree, 1916/17.
Image courtesy of John Alderson

The twelve fallen men from Fir Tree are the ones talked about as their memorial, and in cemeteries where they lay or on foreign memorials.

What of the others who served, the men whose names are not known? What about the men who came back not as the boys and young men who left, not even as heroes, but as men who had experienced some of the most graphic and horrific scenes that they never talked about what they had been through? They came home, some with physical wounds for all to see, but many with psychological wounds hidden from sight, but just as traumatic and scarred for life.

Some of them from Fir Tree who served and survived are known to us and their stories are told below.

Colville Atkinson	Hazelgrove Terrace Fir Tree
George Binks	Harperley Cottage, Harperley Station
Adam Oswald Coates	Harperley Park, Harperley Station
James Alfred Close	3 Howden Head, Fir Tree
Harry Close	Hazelgrove Terrace, Fir Tree
Wilfred Close	Fir Tree, Harperley
Bertrude Dunn	1 Coronation Terrace, Fir Tree
John Corner	Fir Tree, Harperley
Charles Fawcett	Tanfield Lea, Tantobie
James Edward Fitzgerald	Quarry House, Fir Tree
E W Hogarth	Fir Tree, Harperley
Henry Arthur Hogarth	10 East End, Fir Tree
Joseph Tylden Hutchinson	Greenhead Farm
John Herbert Hardy	Greenhead Farm
Thomas Henry Henderson	4 Harperley Terrace, Fir Tree
George Robert Hodgson	High Cold Knot, Fir Tree
John Kearton	Scur House, 2 Hazelgrove Terrace, Fir Tree
Archibald McLeod	Harperley Station, Harperley
Johnathan Mosey	28 First Street, South Moor, Stanley
Arthur Patton	(Jutland Cottage) Fir Tree
Albert Henry Patton	13 Harperley Terrace, Fir Tree
William S. Robinson	Wadley Farm, Fir Tree
Archibald Henry Rouse	Harperley
Joseph Ramshaw	10 Institute Terrace, Fir Tree
Edward Samuels	Fir Tree? (Victoria Row Howden-le-Wear)
George Herbert Stobart	Harperley Park, Fir Tree
John Geoffrey Stobart	Spellow Hill, Knaresborough and Harperley Hall
Richard Trathen	8 Plantation Terrace, Fir Tree
Thomas Trathen	8 Plantation Terrace, Fir Tree
Robert Todd	Institute Terrace, Fir Tree
William Troup	Duke of York Inn, Fir Tree
Joseph Armstrong Usher	The Grove, Fir Tree
Fred Vitty	10 Institute Terrace, Fir Tree
George Vitty	10 Institute Terrace, Fir Tree
John Copper Walkington	Crook
Joseph Nicholas Willis	Coal Bank Farm, Fir Tree
Frank Winchester	10 Institute Terrace, Fir Tree
John Wray	Resident, Harperley Park, Fir Tree

Colville Atkinson

Colville Atkinson was born in 1884 at Thorngill Lodge Hovingham, Yorkshire, to Thomas and Elizabeth Atkinson and he had three younger sisters. His father Thomas was a saddler, and Colville learned his trade from his father.

By the time of the 1911 census he was living as a visitor at The Grove, Fir Tree, Harperley with the Fryer family. Colville's occupation was registered as a self-employed harness & portmanteau maker (heavy leather suit cases), and at that time he was 27 years of age.

On the 22nd October 1913, Colville married Elizabeth Fryer, the daughter of the family he had been staying with in 1911.

Elizabeth and Colville were living at 3 Primrose Crescent, Sunderland, when he volunteered and enlisted in the Royal Field Artillery on the 19th June 1915 and was given the army number 102783. His skills were immediately recognised and he was enlisted as being a 'specially enlisted saddler' and moved straight to Woolwich Barracks. He was quickly assessed and three weeks later was serving in France with "C" Battery, 47th Brigade of the Royal Field Artillery. Colville was quickly promoted to saddler sergeant and received an enhanced pay of 5 shillings a day.

Back home on the 26th January 1916, Elizabeth had moved back to Harperley and gave birth to their son, Colville Dennis Atkinson, but it was not until a year later in February 1917, when his father first saw his boy. Two weeks' leave was again given in January 1918 and Colville served in France for 4 years and 349 days. He was demobilised on the 4th July 1919 and Colville received his three WWI medals, 1914/15 Star, British War Medal and Victory Medal. The family moved back to the Sunderland area where Colville lived until he died in June 1953.

George Binks

Few details are available on George Binks other that his registered address was Harperley Cottage, Harperley Station, and his occupation was a rail wagon mechanic. He enlisted as a gunner in the 5th Reserve Brigade of the Royal Field Artillery, with the number T/251291.

Adam Coates

Adam Coates was born on the 1st February 1896 to Joseph and Mary Ann, in West Hartlepool. He was the youngest of six children and in 1911 was registered as a farm labourer. During WWI he enlisted and joined the Royal Garrison Artillery and served as a gunner with the 101st Siege Battery, number 56765. On enlistment his registered address was Harperley Park, Harperley Station, Fir Tree. After the war he was awarded the Victory Medal and the British War Medal. Adam died in Darlington in December 1981.

James Close

James was born in October 1891 to James and Alice Close in Fir Tree. His father was a hewer in one of the local mines. James followed suit as a colliery engineman and enlisted on the 7th September 1914 at the age of 22 in Bishop Auckland. The following day James and some of his friends from the area travelled to Carlisle to join the 9th Border Regiment, with army number 13608.

After basic training, Private James Close went to France on the 7th September 1915. This was a short tour as in October his regiment caught the train to travel south to Marseilles where they were to embark on to a ship bound for Greece.

The Greek Prime minister sent an envoy to London requesting help for Serbia assisting them defend their country from Bulgarian aggression. This was to be a little known campaign of WWI in Salonika. The men landed there in November 1915, and on the 8th August 1916, James caught malaria and was admitted to the 29th General Hospital in Salonica. James recovered but had many malarial relapses and spent most of his service in and out of hospital until he was transferred to Belmont Road Military Hospital in Liverpool during May 1918. On the 22nd October 1918, Private Close was discharged physically unfit 'due to malaria'. He was awarded a 20% disability allowance for 12 months. One year later, James travelled to Liverpool for his review and he informed them that he had returned to work some 7 months earlier as a colliery engineman for Harperley Collieries. His 20% disability allowance was revoked. He was awarded his three medals, 1914/15 Star, British War Medal and Victory Medal.

Harry Close

Harry Close was born in Fir Tree in October 1885. He married Kate Eve and they had two sons John Henderson Close and James Arnold Close. Harry was a hewer for Harperley Collieries. Private Harry Close enlisted in the Royal Army Medical Corps, with army number 24224. His military records are vague but include the information that he landed in Egypt on the 16th September 1915 and spent most of his service at the 31st General Hospital in Port Said. He was later awarded the 1914/15 Star, British War Medal and Victory Medal.

Wilfred Close

Wilfred Close was born in 1889 to James and Alice Close and brother to James Alfred Close. His occupation before enlistment was a groom. He also served with the 9th Border Regiment so it is reasonable to assume that he enlisted along with his brother and friends in September 1914 and served in Salonika. Private Wilfred Close. with army number 13925, was later awarded the 1914/15 Star, the British War Medal and the Victory Medal.

Bertrude Dunn

Bertie Dunn was born to John George and Margaret in 1895 in Fir Tree. His father was a miner under manager for a local mine owner and Bertie was employed as a fireman. By this it is believed that he was employed at the local brick or pipe yard looking after the kilns.

Bertie served as a gunner, number 5640, in the 106th TF Royal Garrison Artillery. He was awarded the British War Medal.

John Corner

John Corner, recorded in the 1918 Absent Voters' List, is shown as living at Fir Tree, Harperley. This is the same man as John William Corner of 39 Valley Terrace, Howden-le-Wear who served as a Private in the 1st East Yorkshire Regiment, number 15013, and at the end of his service he was awarded the 1914/15 Star, the British Medal and the Victory Medal.

James Fitzgerald

James Fitzgerald lived at Quarry House, Fir Tree, Harperley. In the 1918 Absent Voters' List for Fir Tree, it identifies that he was a 2nd Lieutenant, number 46621, in the 487th Agricultural Labour Corps and the Medal Roll lists that he went to France in May 1918, but nothing else . 2nd Lieutenant Fitzgerald gave a forwarding address of c/o A. H. Harris, The Nothe, Newent, Gloucestershire. He was awarded the Victory Medal and the British War Medal.

Henry Arthur Hogarth

Private Henry Hogarth, number 275237, served with the 7th Durham Light Infantry. According to the 1918 Absent Voters' List, Henry was living at 10 East End, Fir Tree, Harperley. There are no other records available.

Joseph Tylden Hutchinson

Private Joseph Tylden Hutchinson, with the number 4063, served with the Durham Light Infantry, and then with the 460th Company Royal Defence Corps with the number 70972/3. In the Royal Defence Corps he would have seen only home service and was most likely looking after Prisoners of War. In the 1918 Absent Voters' List he was registered as living at Greenhead Farm, Fir Tree. Joseph was awarded the Victory Medal and the British War Medal.

John Hardy

John Herbert Hardy was born in 1896 to John Thomas and Elizabeth Hardy at Salmon Hall, Howden-le-Wear.   On leaving school, he started working originally as a farm labourer and then for Harperley Collieries as a putter. Private John Hardy, number 95503, attested to the 5th Reserves Battalion of the Durham Light Infantry on the 11th January 1916 and, according to his records, he was 5 ft 3 ins tall, had dark brown hair and brown eyes.

John never left England as a result of not completing his basic training as, according to his medical records, he was discharged on the 5th December 1918 being permanently unfit as he suffered from rheumatism at the age of 15.

Thomas Henderson

Thomas was born in 1886 and later married Lina Maude in 1909. They had a daughter called Nancy. The family lived at 4 Harperley Terrace, Fir Tree. On the 5th October 1914, Private Thomas Henderson, number 13332, signed his Attestation Papers and joined the 3rd East Yorkshire Regiment.

He landed in France on the 9th September 1915 and continued serving with the 3rd East Yorkshire Regiment until he was transferred to the 6th Battalion on the 3rd July 1918, and then to the 1st Battalion on the 20th September 1918. On the 8th October, Private Henderson was wounded in action, when something happened to his left hand and he was repatriated back to England. Private Henderson was transferred to the Army Reserve List on the 7th December 1918 when he was discharged on medical grounds. He was awarded a 10% disability allowance and later his three war medals.

George Hodgson

George Robert Hodgson was born in 1885 to William and Betty Hodgson at Newton Pickering, in Yorkshire. His father was a miner and when George left school he worked as a domestic groom.

Several years later he decided to be a miner and the 1911 census records that he was living at High Cold Knot, Fir Tree, and working as an onsetter (coal miner). The onsetter was in charge of the men at the bottom of the mine shaft, in communication with the banksman at the top of the mine. There were several mine shafts near to Cold Knot and Cabin House Wood, close to where George was living.

George had married Ethel and by the time of the 1911 census they had a 13 day old baby boy.

Private George Hodgson enlisted in 1914 in the Royal Army Medical Corps. His number was 24120, and he was posted to the 41st Field Ambulance. He was posted to the Balkans on the 15th September 1915 where he remained for a major part of the war. He was awarded the 1914/15 Star, British War Medal and Victory Medal.

Albert Patton

Albert Patton was born in Fir Tree in 1897 to William and Dinah Patton. In 1911, at the age of 14, Albert was working as a miner pony driver and the family was living at 13 Harperley Terrace. He enlisted on the 11th January 1916 in the Durham Light Infantry, although there are no details of his battalion. Private Patton, number 95491, was discharged on the 20th March 1919 with his records stating:

> 'Discharge V.D.H. Para 392XXVa King's Regulations, (surplus to military requirements not having suffered impairment since entering service)'

His record does not show the award of any medals.

Dinah Patton and her daughter c1910.
Image courtesy of Howden-le-Wear History Society

William Robinson

Private William Stephenson Robinson, number 83722, served with the 4th Northumberland Fusiliers. According to the 1918 Absent Voters' List, he was resident at Wadley Farm, Fir Tree.

Archibald Rouse

Major Archibald Henry Rouse, General Service Corps. The only information available on Archibald is that in the 1918 Absent Voters' List it states that he was registered at Harperley, County Durham.

Edward Samuels

Edward Samuels was born in 1897 to John and Elizabeth Samuels and in 1911 lived at 14 Victoria Row, Howden-le-Wear. He worked in a local pit and, according to the record, he was a member of the 1st Fir Tree Scout Troop. Private Edward Samuels enlisted in the Royal Fusiliers, number GS/112198, and served in the Machine Gun Corps with the number 5813.

Private Edward Samuels, Royal Fusiliers, and Machine Gun Corps.

Image courtesy of John Alderson

George Herbert Stobart

George Stobart was born on 18th February 1871 to William Culley Stobart and Frances Dorothea Wilkinson, at Etherley County Durham. He was educated at Harrow School and the Royal Military Academy, Woolwich, Kent.

Lt. Col. George Herbert Stobart.
Image courtesy of John Alderson

In 1894, he was awarded his commission and went on to fight in the Boer War, gaining the rank of major.

By 1912 he was a Justice of the Peace for County Durham, but was recalled to the colours when WWI broke out. He was mentioned in despatches, and decorated with the Companion Distinguished Service Order in 1915. Promotion followed in 1916 and Lieutenant Colonel Stobart continued in the service of the War Office until the end of the war. He was working with the Director of Graves Registration and Enquiries.

Hay time at Witton Tower, Witton-le-Wear, in 1916 with the Stobart Family. Lt. Col. George Herbert Stobart is in the left background with light hat. He must have been on leave.
Image courtesy of John Alderson

In 1919, he was invested as a Commander, Order of the British Empire (CBE), and was awarded the 1914/15 Star, the British and the Victory medals.

In 1920, George was in the service of 6th Battalion of the Durham Light Infantry. He was living at Harperley Park, Harperley, Fir Tree. By 1924, George was a Deputy Lieutenant of County Durham and in 1925 was given the honour of being the High Sheriff of County Durham.

In 1925, George was again promoted to Colonel of the 151st Durham Light Infantry Brigade and between 1925 and 1929 he held the office of Aide-de-Camp to H.M. King George V. In 1930, he gained the rank of Honorary Colonel in the service of the 6th Battalion, Durham Light Infantry.

George Stobart died at Helme Park on the 27th May 1943 at the aged of 72.

Richard Trathen

Richard Trathen was born in North Skelton, Yorkshire, in 1896 to Walter and Mary Trathen. By 1911 he was living at home in 8 Plantation Terrace, Fir Tree, Harperley Station. Richard worked for Harperley Collieries alongside his father and brothers and his occupation was a pony driver.

He enlisted into Royal Navy, number SS116153, on the 14th September 1916 and worked as a Stoker on *H.M.S. St Vincent*. She was a dreadnought class battleship of 20,000 tons. Richard was awarded the British and Victory War Medals.

Richard Todd

Private Richard Todd served with the Durham Light Infantry, and then in the Labour Corps. He is registered in the 1918 Absent Voters' List as living at Institute Terrace, Fir Tree. After the war Richard was awarded the Victory and British War Medals.

William Troup

According to the 1918 Absent Voters' List, William Troup was living at the Duke of York Inn at Fir Tree. After enlistment with the Royal Horse Artillery, he arrived in France on 7th December 1914. He served throughout the war and was awarded the 1914/15 Star, British medal and Victory Medal.

Joseph Usher

Private Joseph Usher served with the Army Service Corps, number M/2191909. The Absent Voters' List shows that in 1918 he was registered as living at The Grove, Fir Tree. Joseph was awarded The Victory and British War Medal.

George Vitty

George Vitty was born in 1890 at Phoenix Row, Etherley, Bishop Auckland to William and Priscilla Vitty. George worked for Harperley Collieries as a putter with his father and brother Fred, who later was killed in France. Private George Vitty, number 14649, was a bugler with the 14th Service Battalion of the Durham Light Infantry.

Some of George's story was told in the section on his brother Fred and we left George when he had been evacuated to a Field Ambulance Station on the 19th December 1915, as a result of a phosgene gas attack. Shortly after this, George was given leave to return to England, which he refused, stating that, although he was classed as unfit to fight, it was his duty to stay with the 14th and his comrades and brother.

Private George Vitty, Bugler "D" Coy., 14th Battalion D.L.I.
Image courtesy of John Alderson

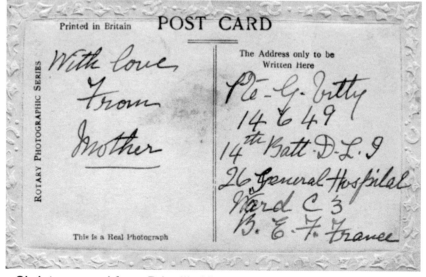

Christmas card from Priscilla Vitty to her son, George, after the gas attack in 1915. *Image courtesy of John Alderson*

In January 1916, he returned to his Company. Although still unfit for fighting, he stated he could fetch, carry, repair trenches and provide hot food for his mates in "D" Company.

He eventually regained his health and returned to the front line. During March, near Ypres, the German army called a ceasefire in order to recover their wounded servicemen. At the same time, British stretcher bearers left their trenches and George was returning to the British line carrying the rear of a stretcher with an injured allied soldier when the German machine guns opened fire. The stretcher bearer to the front fell dead and at the same time George was hit in the right shoulder. The already wounded casualty was hit again and George, with one arm, pulled him back to the allied first line of trenches. They both received first aid in the trench by the field ambulance medics and then were evacuated. George was transported to Number 26 General Hospital, Etaples, where his right arm was amputated at the shoulder. The hospital was on the River Canche and George was repatriated by ship. He was admitted into Ward 1, at the Richmond Hospital in Dublin but, as this was the time of the Sinn Fein Rebellion, he was quickly sent back to Edenhall in Cumbria where he sent a postcard home on the 16th September.

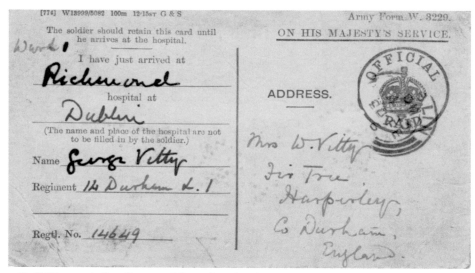

Rail Warrant, for George Vitty, for the family to visit him in Richmond Hospital, Dublin.

Image courtesy of John Alderson

George was then moved to Floors Castle in Kelso, in Scotland, and again he wrote a postcard home on the 23rd October 1916 with a note on the back:

"Will not be home this week, my arm did not come, Geo."

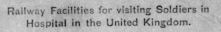

Railway Facilities for visiting Soldiers in Hospital in the United Kingdom.

FREE WARRANTS.—If the soldier is in a *grave condition*, the Medical Officer in Charge of the Hospital is authorised to issue a Free Railway Warrant to *one* relation to visit him, provided that the relation is not in a position to pay the fare.

Should the Medical Officer in Charge of the Hospital telegraph to the next-of-kin to proceed to the hospital without delay, a refund of the cost of the railway fare will be made under the condition laid down in para. I.

CHEAP TICKETS.—Medical Officers in Charge of Hospitals are authorised to issue Vouchers for Cheap Tickets, which allow the double journey at the single fare, to soldiers' relations under the following conditions:—

    A. That the journey is not less than 30 miles in the outward direction.

    B. That tickets will be issued for not more than two adults, or one adult and two children under 12.

Only one visit is allowed in each case, unless the Medical Officer in Charge of the Hospital should consider a second visit desirable.

N.B.—Applications for Vouchers should be addressed to the Medical Officers-in-Charge of Hospitals, to whose discretion the issue is entirely left.

Private George Vitty whilst convalescing with two unknown servicemen. George is seated in army uniform.
Image courtesy of John Alderson

From here he was transferred a final time to convalesce at Guisborough Hall, North Yorkshire. George was given a medical discharge on 8th June 1917 as he was '*No longer physically fit for war service*' owing to a gunshot wound and right arm amputation. He was 26 years and 6 months old, height 5 ft 5 ins, complexion fair, eyes blue, hair brown, marks or scars "less right arm". He was described as "*A steady and sober man*" with 2 years' 274 days' service.

George received his silver war badge to prove he had served his country and was unfit for service. He was also awarded the 1914/15 Star, British War Medal and Victory Medal.

In 1917, George was awarded a 100% disablement pension. After twelve months it was reviewed, when it was decided that it was too high and so it was reduced to 70%. In 1922, George joined BLESMA (British Limbless Ex-Service Men's Association) which helped wounded and disabled men return with help to as near normal a life as could be expected.

After the war, George worked with his father and the scouts learning to come to terms with his disability, and then in 1923 got a job as a postman delivering and collecting mail from Harperley station. In 1927 he married Nellie Stephenson from Wolsingham. Although George was working and running the Boy Scout Troop, he spent time in Sherburn House Hospital, owing to the ongoing effects of the 1915 phosgene gas attack. During these times in hospital, the village pulled together looking after his young family whilst his wife did the postal round.

In 1952, BLESMA conducted a survey among some 4,000 members and, after a medical, George had his disability pension raised to 90% and, after 38 years, he received a back payment of £900.

George retired from the post office in 1960 aged 70 years, and five years later retired as scout master from the 2nd Fir Tree Scout Troop. He spent most of his retirement in his garden growing fruit and vegetables for the family and on Saturdays going on the train to Middlesbrough to watch the team play football. Every year he would travel alone to Edinburgh on the train to see the Military Tattoo. George Vitty died on the 24th December 1979 after a full and eventful life.

George Vitty, with Harperley Station Master, in the late 1920s.
Image courtesy of John Alderson

Joseph Willis

Joseph Nicholas Willis was born in 1896 to Joseph and Eliza Willis in Lanchester, County Durham. In 1911 he and his family were living at Grey's Well, Tow Law, and he was registered as being a coal miner. He enlisted with the 5th Reserves Battalion of the Durham Light Infantry, number 95497, and the 1918 Absent Voters' List shows that the family had moved to Coal Bank Farm, Fir Tree, Harperley. Private Joseph Willis was discharged from the army at the end of the war and was awarded the Victory and British War Medal.

Frank Winchester

Frank Winchester was born in North Woolwich, Essex, in 1889 and in 1901 was working as a butcher's apprentice. He joined the 9th Queen's Royal Lancers in 1911, number 3462L/3462, and moved to Stockton-on-Tees.

In May 1912, Frank married Eleanor Vitty of Fir Tree at Guisborough in North Yorkshire, where she was in service to a local family. Later that year their son Frank was born.

When war broke out, Frank was very quickly on the front line and on the 21st August 1914, he and the 9th Lancers arrived in France as part of the British Expeditionary Force. Eleanor and young Frank moved back to 10 Institute Terrace, Fir Tree, for the duration of the war.

Private Frank Winchester, 9th Queen's Royal Lancers.
Image courtesy of John Alderson

Frank served throughout the war and was demobilized to the army reserve on the 22nd March 1919 and returned to Eleanor at Fir Tree. Shortly afterwards they moved to Guisborough, North Yorkshire. He was awarded the14 Star with Clasp and Roses, the Victory and British War Medals.

❖ *BIBLIOGRAPHY*

This book was not produced as a serious academic work. The researchers are all people with a hobby that they have learned to love and are not professional historians or researchers. In acknowledging this, it should be noted that systematic research methods have been used by everyone involved, resulting in a book which has given so much satisfaction.

Many books, websites, pamphlets and leaflets have been used by the researchers of this book. There has also been a high level of information obtained from relatives of the families mentioned in the book: this has been taken at face value and much has been verified by secondary research. All of the information included in the book has been used in the belief that it is accurate. Images have all been accredited to individuals or institutions and appropriate permissions received to use them. This has been a learning experience for all involved and one that has increased knowledge and given a great deal of joy and the feeling of achievement.

If anybody wishes to obtain information about how the research was carried out, please contact Howden-le-Wear History Society by email: Howden-le-Wearhistorysociety@hotmail.co.uk

❖ *Howden-le-Wear Local History Society*

The Society was formed in March 1995 with the aim of recording and preserving the village heritage for future generations. In the past there have been very successful exhibitions and displays and the Society holds a large archive of local information which has full public access. Several books have been published about the village and its history.

The present two year WWI project, funded by the Heritage Lottery Fund, was established at the end of 2013 and those with an interest in this period have freely given their time and energy to the development of this book.

Back row (l to r): Tom Parkin, Irene Brian, Kathleen Parkin, Christine Gibson, John Alderson
Front row: (l to r): David Marshall, Anne Yuill, Chris Gibson, Joan Potts.
Absent from photograph: Mike Abbott, Alan Brian, Frances Ann Johnson, Helen Morton.

❖ INDEX